Gallery of Clouds

RACHEL EISENDRATH

nyrb **New York Review Books** New York

This is a New York Review Book

published by The New York Review of Books

435 Hudson Street, New York, NY 10014

www.nyrb.com

Library of Congress Cataloging-in-Publication Data
Names: Eisendrath, Rachel, author.
Title: Gallery of clouds / Rachel Eisendrath.
Description: New York City : New York Review Books, 2021.
Identifiers: LCCN 2020016141 (print) | LCCN 2020016142
    (ebook) | ISBN 9781681375434 (hardcover) |
    ISBN 9781681375441 (ebook)
Subjects: CSH: Books and reading. | Literature—Appreciation.
Classification: LCC Z1003 .E355 2021 (print) | LCC Z1003
    (ebook) | DDC 028/.9—dc23
LC record available at https://lccn.loc.gov/2020016141
LC ebook record available at https://lccn.loc.gov/2020016142

ISBN 978-1-68137-543-4
Available as an electronic book; ISBN 978-1-68137-544-1

Printed in the United States of America on acid-free paper.

1 2 3 4 5 6 7 8 9 10

Preface

New York City, April 2021

I DIED AND THEN FOUND MYSELF walking across a large, green field. You might think heaven would be overflowing with rare flowers and exotic birds, but this meadow was just plain city grass mixed with dandelions. Some taller weeds grew along the periphery, where the mower hadn't been able to reach. A few sparrows and pigeons, perhaps slightly fatter and sleeker than those to which I was accustomed, hopped about here and there. Some trees. The meadow might almost have been in Central Park.

Soon, I could see in the distance a small group of people, who were sitting in wicker lawn chairs beneath a cluster of large oaks. A woman was talking, and a few men were listening, leaning back in postures of attentive ease. One of them had his fingers interlaced behind his head, his legs crossed. Something about the

position of their heads indicated their intelligence. I found, to my surprise, that I wasn't at all scared or shy as I approached them; I merely wanted to join their conversation. The only desirable kind of heaven, I remembered reading somewhere, is one in which you can contemplate this life. And these people seemed to be actively discussing this life.

Now I was standing before them. The light was playing on the pattern of the woman's dress, and my eyes could not at first sort out what was light and what was her dress.

She paused in her talk and looked at me.

I thought: —*Oh.* —*Thank God.* —*There are gay women in heaven.* I did not even feel daunted that she was Virginia Woolf.

The men, curious who had drawn this glance from their friend, turned then to look at me. But, already, Virginia Woolf's glance was making me bold. Already, I was growing older, climbing up through the ages of myself so that, as she watched me, I slowly regained the age I actually was, which was close to her age. But it was as if I had drawn those earlier ages up with me and so was now all the ages of myself at the same time. Improbably, without preamble or warning, I found myself telling a rabbinic story about a man who dies and dreams that he finds God. God is sitting at the far end of a room, where He is reading the Torah by candlelight. "What's wonderful about the story," I informed Virginia Woolf, "is that God is studying the pages of His own life! Wouldn't He already know everything that was in that book?"

Virginia Woolf glanced delightedly at her friends and said to me, "But what is in that folder? Have you brought me a gift?"

I realized then that I was carrying my manuscript under my arm and promptly held it out to her.

This was the moment, surely, to introduce my book. Her eyes were focused on me. They—her eyes—were two theatergoers that had settled deeply into their plush seats and were now looking expectantly at my face.

But what should I say?

In the tension of that moment, two possible approaches arose in my mind, one academic, the other personal:

1) *Academic.* It is an analogy so common that it is hard to recognize as an analogy: that a work of literature is like a subjectivity. Both operate, largely, in a verbal medium. A book exists in words;

I think in words. Moreover, a book is like a subjectivity in that it can—or it can seem to—take in observations about the world, perceive itself, double back on itself, reevaluate itself, be subject to varying interpretations, refuse to pin itself down. Collections of lyric poetry in particular often explicitly claim to locate the reader within the mind of the author.

The structure of a book can, therefore, offer a kind of implicit theory of subjectivity. Some of the most famous collections of lyric poems, like Petrarch's *Canzoniere*, are written in a form that is fragmented. Petrarch first called the collection *Rerum vulgarium fragmenta* (Fragments of Vernacular Things), and the first poem describes itself as "*rime sparse*" (scattered rhymes). These articulations might suggest a theory of mind: that there was once something whole that has been disrupted, dispersed—a paradise lost, a childhood lost, an intimacy with God lost, a time before desire struck (separating the world into subjects and wanted objects) also lost.

So what kind of mind is my book? Although this book, like a collection of lyric poems (despite being prose), is written in pieces, in a non-narrative mode, it is not written in fragments, shards, or scattered rhymes.

No unity has been lost because there never was any unity.

That is why this is a book of clouds. Clouds are ephemeral

moments of light and color that stay still only as long as you look at them, but then—as soon as your mind wanders—change into something else.

2) *Personal.* It is said, rightly, that books can save your life. Surely, they can do so in many ways—in as many ways, maybe, as there are readers, as there are hours, as there are apartments, as there are chairs, as there are lamps, as there are cups of coffee, as there are books. In my case, ever since I could remember, I had been inexplicably anxious, given even to a kind of experience of nonbeing (as though that were possible). There must have been reasons for why, from an early age, I was beset with fear and with the sensation that the world, or even I myself, was not entirely solid. It may have been that my father had left us, unsettling my first sense of things; or that my mother then had no one and despaired of her ability to support us; or that perhaps there had once been a certain unspeakable finger that had known me before, as Shakespeare's Adonis says, I had known myself. Who's to say? But, surely, even the basic arrangements of existence, the universal rules under which we all live (the inevitability of death, to begin), are so strange that no further reason is needed for anyone to feel perplexed and unsolid—never mind (for now) all the other disasters that can wrack a human on her journey from one shore to

the other. For me, the solution to this perplexity—or, since no solution is really possible, the orientation toward psychic survival or even toward joy—came in the most unlikely way possible: It was, incredibly, through reading that I was able to find a place for my consciousness. (*Incredibly* because we have been trained to think that intellectual life and well-being are two separable things.) This place for my consciousness was a kind of Arcadia that was necessarily both a freedom from the pressures of a largely unsparing reality and a reflection on those pressures, a way of inhabiting at the same time both myself (whatever that is) and also another person (whatever that is), a way of drawing in history (whatever that is), a way of thinking in a mode of sufficient complexity and suppleness that my mind felt real and also could whir along with a certain lightness, in an as-if mode that is the single ground rule of fiction. If fiction is anything, claimed Sir Philip Sidney (about whom we will have much to discuss), it must be that fiction is that which is so and not so at the same time. In his words, it is that which "never lieth" because it never claims to tell the truth. In this unlikely way, I became a reader, one who read and read and read (and still reads), and eventually became a professor of Renaissance poetry (which is what I am now). The clouds in my Arcadia, the one I found and the one I made, hold light and color. They take on the forms of other things: a cat, the sea, my grandmother, the gesture of a teacher I loved, a friend, a girlfriend, a ship at sail, my mother. These clouds stay still only as long as I look at them, and then they change.

But I did not say any of those words to Virginia Woolf.

Instead, just as I opened my mouth to speak, she smiled at me with her eyes. Truly, there should be a separate grammar—a Grammar of the Hypothetical—for all the questions and answers that can be exchanged, or might be exchanged, at such a moment when everything seems to pause in the interchange of a significant glance, "when first your eye I eyed," as Shakespeare says in sonnet 104, where the "eye"s and "I"s bounce back and forth against each other. Suddenly, standing before Virginia Woolf, holding out my manuscript, I found that the present moment included a seemingly infinite number of possible presents, and possible futures, all of which could happen and also, most likely, wouldn't happen. Each movement of her eyes made my eyes move, which made her eyes move, and so on. The possibilities seemed, for a moment, endless. I was looking into a new world—her eyes— moist globes, suspended in space like planets, but with that slight quiver and charge and receptivity and assertiveness that belong to what's living...

But then the moment had passed. She had taken hold of my manuscript. And she was looking down at it, and opening it, and soon she began to read.

IT'S VERY IMPORTANT where you read such books, and under
what conditions, and where you first find the volumes, or even
who hands them to you. C. S. Lewis said that the best way to read
an Italian romance—of which Sir Philip Sidney's *Arcadia* is a
first cousin on the family's English side—is for eight hours a day
in a room by the sea while recovering from a minor illness. That
advice is exactly right because one can't place workaday demands
on these books: theirs is the realm of long days; of wonder; of
unfilled space and time; of wandering passages between an afternoon nap and waking; of attentive receptivity; of the soft blue

ocean on a map that induces fantasies about places you know next to nothing about; of sunlight shifting over a wall beside your bed. Jorge Luis Borges says that the meaning of some long books lies in their length, and these books are of that kind. These books have little plot, and that little plot has little shape; the books are episodic, following what Northrop Frye once called an "and-then" structure (or nonstructure). These books are long, therefore, not in order to complete any discernible trajectory or arc, nor to create an illusion of completeness, but rather to make you feel that the adventures could go on forever, that there is no intrinsic reason why these books should ever have to stop, and that, as Borges also says, even after these books have ended at some more or less arbitrary spot, you will feel that they are still, somewhere, going on. Like the *Arabian Nights* or *In Search of Lost Time*, these books do not fight off death; rather, they forestall it. They do so by increasing the thickness of time, which maybe also means that they are sometimes a little boring—in a luxuriant way. Their air is thicker than air; it is golden and sun-drenched and heavy. *I will get up and do what I am supposed to do*, these books say, *but not quite yet*.

In this particular case, I had ordered only one volume, but two green hardback books, their spines slightly faded from sunlight, had arrived in the mail: volumes I and II of a 1963 Cambridge reprint of Albert Feuillerat's 1912 edition of *The Prose Works of*

Sir Philip Sidney. The spines of the volumes were stiff and softly cracked when I opened them. Unfolding the package, I found this note from the seller inside:

Dear Miss Eisendrath,

    These books have stood side by side for many years since I left graduate school. Please accept vol 2 as a gift. Besides, I left the land of nymphs and shepherds long ago.

R. C. W——

The script was a wavering cursive, from the generation of my grandmothers; the last sentence was written in iambic heptameter. The note evoked not only the geographical distance of the previous owner but also the gap of time: a period in graduate school many years ago, and then untold years on the shelf during which these two volumes had stood together as witness to the slow unfolding of their previous reader's life. Now he was no longer young, and these same volumes lay in my hands. It was as if the books were not just about romance, but had themselves come from the world of romance. Virginia Woolf describes a similar experience in 1932 when finding her volumes of the *Arcadia* on the bottom shelf, where they seemed to have sunk "as if by their own weight": "We like to feel," she writes, "that the present is not all; that other hands have been before us, smoothing the leather until the corners are rounded and blunt, turning the pages until they are yellow and dog's-eared. We like to summon before us the ghosts of those old readers who have read their *Arcadia* from this very copy." The *Arcadia* has a peculiar power to produce such conditions of readership: the book starts to seem like some object from within its own pages, a wondrous object that has its own sprawling story to tell of distant places and long-ago times and hard travel.

A teacher of mine had once made such books attractive to me not by bringing them close and making them seem modern, but, with wistful love and rigor, by holding them at a distance—where they had gleamed darkly like someone else's jewels. He had once been mocked for arguing that the place of fairyland in Edmund Spenser's 1590 *The Faerie Queene*—another English cousin—was *real*: it was, he said, for so Spenser had said. Fairyland was the New World, a real place that in the late sixteenth century still glowed in the half-light of European longing. But if my teacher

was mocked, what did he care? He spent his days bent over old maps and manuscripts in his sixteenth-floor apartment in Chicago. It was said that he had two apartments: one to hold books; the other, next door, to hold books and a bed. Poised over Lake Michigan, with the city sprawled beneath him, his apartment might as well have been the peak of Machu Picchu. He seemed to me to be a character of romance himself. Imagine erudition illuminated by wonder. He would travel to the places he wrote about: for his book on trade and romance, he had journeyed in bits and pieces along much of the Silk Road. Once, he sent me one of my chapter drafts with his comments from a hotel in the Alps of Switzerland, where, he said, the staff always saved a particular room for him each year. I wondered at the brown envelope, which bore the handwriting of the concierge, as I would have a rock from the moon or a ring of the sultan. It was this teacher who told me that the most amazing magic that the fantastical pages of romance produce is this: that the real is what is to be wondered at.

In the case of Sidney's *Arcadia*, the book writes such conditions of wonder-filled reading into its own pages. Sidney describes in the opening dedication the circumstance of his very first reader, his sister, the Countess of Pembroke, for whom he composed the romance:

> For indeed, for severer eyes it is not, being but a trifle, and that triflingly handled. Your dear self can best witness the manner, being done in loose sheets of paper, most of it in your presence, the rest, by sheets, sent unto you, as fast as they were done. In sum, a young head, not so well stayed as I would it were (and shall be when God will), having many fancies begotten in it, if it had not been in some way delivered, would have grown a monster, & more sorry might I be that they came in, than that they got out.

Conjured before us: loose sheets of paper that Sidney handed to his sister one after the other, the ink still wet, as soon as he had composed them—almost like letters written from the land of his imagination, while the events he fantasized were just then unfolding in his mind.

This condition of domestic familiarity and knowing humor endowed with humanity the rhetorically elaborate arabesques of Sidney's pen. I imagine that he and his sister must have wondered at themselves, as my family wondered at itself living such a different kind of life in a one-bedroom apartment in Washington, DC, turning to themselves as objects of fantasy that were also real: *How is it possible*, his sister might have asked, *that I am the Countess of Pembroke?* In her ermine-lined gown, she was already for herself a character of fiction. As he was for himself—and as he was for others. He was already so fantastical that when he died at the age of thirty-one, Adonis-like, after having been shot in the leg at the Battle of Zutphen, it took almost nothing to render him a semifictional ideal. Scores of poems appeared eulogizing this fallen shepherd. Fulke Greville, his lifelong friend, wrote a biography. His funeral was one of the most glittering that the glittering Elizabethan period had known: we still have thirty-two engravings that show the long procession with his coffin; they were once attached in one continuous sheet so that they could be turned on pins to make a moving procession. But for all the elaborate staging of Elizabethan courtly life, it had been in the domestic sphere of intimacy, first on the family estate at Penshurst, and then on his sister's estate at Wilton, that Sidney discovered how the world of art and fantasy could help him deal with himself: "I readily confess that I am often more melancholy than either my age or my activities demand; but I have fully proved by experience that I am never less liable to moods of melancholy than while I am pitting my weak mental powers against some difficult challenge," he wrote in a Latin letter of 1574. His father's secretary noted that Sidney could not endure idleness. His sister would have known what that meant, and perhaps also experienced it in herself: *Yes*, she may have thought, arranging for fresh pages and good ink, *more room out than in*. Space and time were needed—air—light—expansion. And a reader.

•

The windows of the apartment building where I grew up faced west. As the late afternoon gave way to evening, my family talked and cooked and argued against a backdrop of clouds, an astonishing drama of colors that concentrated into pools of orange or red or purple, until finally dark descended and the sky seemed to disappear into itself. Each sunset was different, and each was amazing, and each seemed to erase my memory of the one that came before it.

On summer nights, even after it was fully dark, the girls who jumped rope in front of the apartment building could still be heard, keeping time by clapping and stamping and rhyming. Sometimes, I would go downstairs to sit on the low wall that circled the driveway and watch them. The girls skipped double dutch, having learned the trick of that complex synchronization, which is to get the rhythm into their bodies before jumping into the ropes. Standing to one side of the swinging ropes, which whipped against the sidewalk at each rotation, the girls would rock their lean or big bodies back and forth, so that they were already moving in the right way by the time they jumped into the ropes. When these girls had arguments or fought, they stood very close to each other, with their faces nearly touching, almost as though they were about to kiss, and then they would insult each other, accentuating each phrase by moving their heads to one side and then the other. Here was a good school for language because the insult either had timing, flair, style—or it did not. There could be no mewling. And even if no one mistook me for being the kind of girl who could be expected to behave fully like a girl, still, occasionally, even my turn would come to jump into the ropes, or to fight, and then it was imperative that I not flinch.

And I did not.

•

A dark room inside a dark house. On one dark wood wall, a dark rug with a pattern of dark reds. A dark portrait of an ancestor in a dark gown who looks darkly from the height of his dark past and of his own rigidly trained posture. A room that is without bookcases but that is, itself, somehow like a bookcase. A small window that lets through a narrow shaft of light—through which float upward strangely pristine bits of golden dust. The faint smell of a swept fireplace. When entering this room, everyone over sixteen years old stiffens and becomes like a portrait of herself.

It is perhaps hard for us now to imagine how closely the English aristocracy identified with their family estates, almost as if they and their parents and their grandparents were made, like their houses, of the stone and wood from the local quarry and copse. An ancestor had risen out of this ground, and then had sunk back into it. The name of the place was often the name of the family: Gloucester, Essex,

Albany, Northumberland. The great house, with its many additions, was the family's strange body. Even when the person traveled elsewhere, he felt as though he carried this place on his very body, like the famous second-millennium hippopotamus, which, in a glass case in the Metropolitan Museum of Art in New York, bears on its surface line drawings of the river reeds in which it once had hidden from the hot Egyptian sun. So, too, among the English aristocracy, figure and ground were impossible fully to distinguish: the place is the person—or at least so the person thought.

•

Putting my hands on either side of the podium: *Literature*, I announced to the class, *is a history of retrospection*. Italian romance—*it is well known*—rose to a peak in the late fifteenth and early sixteenth centuries, at a time when the world this romance described of feudal warriors and great Eastern journeys was waning—if it ever really existed at all. A work like Matteo Maria Boiardo's *Orlando innamorato*, a *great* Italian romance, the precursor of Ludovico Ariosto's *Orlando furioso*, a more famous and *no less great* Italian romance, is a long and affectionate look backward at this lost world. The intellectual historian Hans Blumenberg once said that when he imagined Homer, he imagined someone preoccupied with a world going out of existence. Such worlds shimmered in the imagination just before they disappeared from reality. Johan Huizinga uncovered this dynamic in his 1919 *The Autumn of the Middle Ages*, where he describes with remarkable vividness the last cultural flourishing of the fourteenth and fifteenth centuries in France and the Netherlands: church bells (known by household names like Fat Jacqueline) reverberated through the streets; ostentatious nobles, dressed in fur-lined robes, sauntered by lepers with rattles; and the most intimate matters of life were "glitteringly and cruelly public." The quality of vivid retrospection is especially important to romance. If epic is about *doing, acting, overcoming, singing*—romance is about *waiting, enduring, receiving, listening*. Yes, but not so simply, because romance also shows that one end of this dichotomy, followed far enough, eventually loops back around and becomes the other end, albeit in an altered way, so that *waiting, enduring, receiving, listening* turns out to be a form of *doing, acting, overcoming, singing...*

Most students were not exactly listening to me, but rather watching my face. They felt that slower sense of time that obtains in a lecture room, that viscous quality of air. After the first hour, the room had become like a pool. Except for my voice, which was pleasant enough as *sound*, it was weirdly quiet underwater. Limbs moved so slowly. When my voice suddenly rose now into a more pointy, rapid, and somehow also *needy* set of notes that flagged *the professor has just asked a question*, it was as though the students were suddenly jerked out of this warm and kindly water. How cold the air was. But then they saw that I had already moved on to my next point and that I was again fully engrossed in whatever it was I was saying, and, being sensitive and largely courteous people, the students nodded encouragingly.

•

In the sixteenth century, the question of doing or not doing, of the demands of the world versus the call of literature, was often phrased in terms of the active versus the contemplative life, *vita activa* versus *vita contemplativa*—business versus leisure,

negotium versus *otium*. Of course, that one could have a conversation about this question at all already implies a measure of contemplation. For such thoughts about how to live one's life, or for what, have nothing to say to the demands of the day, as Sir Andrew Aguecheek inadvertently implies in Shakespeare's *Twelfth Night*: "What is *pourquoi*? Do, or not do?" Theodor W. Adorno positions this impasse as a condition of art, which is helpless before the question "What are you for?"

Sidney's education, first at Shrewsbury School, later at Christ Church, Oxford, and finally on a tour through the courts of continental Europe, was considered preparatory for active involvement in the world's affairs. He was the eldest son of two illustrious parents: His mother was Mary Dudley, Queen Elizabeth's lady-in-waiting. His father was Sir Henry Sidney, three-time Lord Deputy of Ireland. Deeply involved in the violent struggle for domination of Protestants over Catholics, these aristocrats fully expected that their prodigiously talented son would play his part. Philip *must*—one elder after another was called in to make this point—make good the training he had received. So said, for example, his intimate mentor Hubert Languet, a fifty-some-year-old French Protestant and humanist diplomat, who, like Sidney, was in Paris during the horrifying 1572 Saint Bartholomew's Day Massacre, when, during the Wars of Religion, thousands of French Protestants were slaughtered by mobs. In a letter written from Vienna, he warned the eighteen-year-old Sidney that he must

> be careful not to let your thirst for learning and acquiring information lead you into danger. You remember how often and how solemnly you have promised me to be cautious. If you fail in this, I shall charge you with a breach of the contract that is between us, and you will be forced to confess that you have broken the terms of our friendship. To offend me is of little consequence, but reflect how grievously you would be sinning against your excellent Father, who has placed all his hopes in you, and who, being now in the flower of life, expects to see the full harvest of all those virtues which your character promises so largely to produce.

The danger was not just that the young Sidney was traveling through Catholic country, but that he was losing himself in his literary studies. Several such warnings appear in the letters of Languet: "You must consider your condition in life, how soon you will have to tear yourself from your literary leisure, and therefore the short time which you still have should be devoted entirely to such things as are most essential." Languet sympathizes with Sidney's desire for study, and even shares it himself, but advises resistance. It's all well to imitate Cicero's letters for "the very important matter they contain," but one must not lose oneself in too close an involvement with their style. This literary young man must realize that books are opened only in order, finally, that they be shut.

For much of the Renaissance, the great model of the philosopher-as-statesman was Cicero, who gave form both in his deeds and in his words to this ideal. He had maintained a high level of political involvement even after the rise to power of his political enemy Mark Antony, who was responsible for his execution in 43 BCE. In his *On Obligations*, Cicero acknowledges the great impulse we may feel to withdraw from public life. The hunger for pure speculation and the impulse to search for the truth may even come "closest to the essentials of human nature," but this impulse must be kept subordinate to our most basic obligation: public service. We must not "devote too much energy and effort on matters which are not merely arcane and taxing, but also unnecessary." Obey the call to action, which leads outward into the world; resist the impulse to pure speculation, which ever "turns in on itself."

But such values were hardly immune to challenge in the Renaissance. As early as 1345, Petrarch criticized Cicero for giving a false appearance to what may have been just a desire for attention and worldly glory. Petrarch even addressed a letter to him, as though this ancient figure who had died 1,400 years before were an intimate friend. "Oh," he wrote to Cicero, "how much better it would have been, especially for a philosopher, to have grown old peacefully in the country, meditating, as you write somewhere, on that everlasting life and not on this transitory existence; how much better for you never to have held such offices, never to have yearned for triumphs, never to have had any Catilines to inflate your ego."

But Sidney, as he had been trained to do, took his place in Elizabeth's court. He fulfilled a diplomatic mission to Prague in 1577, but in 1579 he opposed too outspokenly the Earl of Oxford's support of Elizabeth's match to the French Catholic François, Duc d'Anjou. Oxford challenged him to a duel (or he challenged Oxford); the queen intervened; Sidney was banished from court. When he was finally allowed back, she gave him nothing important to do. To have ignored the unspoken rules of royal power had been worse than naive: *Don't forget that, on a chessboard, the queen can move in any direction she likes.* (So remarked Sidney scholar Roger Kuin, who was sitting in front of me at a conference, turning around in his seat in order to respond to an unintelligible remark of mine concerning Elizabeth's poem "Ah, silly Pug.") It was during this period of semi-exile from the inner circles of power that Sidney wrote much of his literary work: *The Defence of Poesy*, the *Arcadia*, and *Astrophil and Stella*—major works that changed the course of English literature, but that pass almost without mention in his letters. Some critics portray this six-year period in which Sidney was barred from the court as a period of stymie and "acute frustration." They quote Greville's claim that, for Sidney, "his end was not writing, even while he wrote; nor his knowledge molded for tables or schools, but both his wit and understanding bent upon his heart to make himself and others, not in words or opinion, but in life and action, good and great." For Greville, as for many others in Sidney's world, a writer's purpose should be worldly action. And so Sidney himself says—at least sometimes. In a 1578 letter to Languet, for example, Sidney writes: "I have not as yet done anything worthy of me."

Yet in his writings, intimations also emerge of other notions of virtue that are less directly action-based. In this same 1578 letter to Languet, for example, Sidney questions the idea that the best kind of study is that which can be turned most readily to practical purpose:

> Let us see whether we are not giving a beautiful but false appearance to our splendid errors. For while the mind is thus, as it were, drawn out of itself, it cannot turn its powers inward for thorough self-examination; to which employment no labor that men can undertake is any way to be compared.

The highest activity, here at least, is that of self-examination. But Sidney doesn't maintain his position for long—motion, not fixity, is his aim. As if uncomfortable with any position that threatens to rigidify into a single didactic stance, Sidney then shifts his tone and, as if it were all a joke, breaks into a kind of smile:

> Do you not see that I am cleverly playing the stoic? Yea, and I shall be a cynic too, unless you reclaim me. Wherefore, if you please, prepare yourself to attack me. I have now pointed out the field of battle, and I openly declare war against you.

Perhaps the position that there's nothing more valuable than self-exploration is not Sidney's position, after all, but only the position of a kind of character to whom Sidney has given voice.

Does Sidney mean what he says? The argument doesn't come to rest: Sidney puts the idea forward and then withdraws it, in an almost flirtatious manner, as if eliciting his reader, in this case the older humanist Languet, to follow him, to oppose him—in some manner, to join him in the field of thought and investigation.

•

My stepfather lay on the couch and watched the light moving on the wall and talked to me at length about the wisdom of silence. I liked to pretend I was sick so that I could stay home, too, so we often spent the days together. On some days he dressed and went out to look for a job, but then generally went back to lying on the couch. He wore an undershirt and a towel wrapped firmly around his waist, samurai-style. For a while, he was a telemarketer, before that a house painter. He dressed carefully for these jobs, matching his socks by holding them up against his shirt, and then performed his given tasks with a meticulous and craftsmanly care that was totally incongruous with what he had been hired to do. On certain days despair came over him. But then his despair would pass, and there appeared a light in his eyes, which maybe had been there all along, and this light in his eyes eventually led us back out into the sun. And then he was shaking his head at his absurdity, and laughing, and sitting on the couch with all of us, and we were talking, and eating, and reading, and listening to music on the record player. And there arose again a palace of splendor in poverty, which, like a miraculous view in the distance, appeared and disappeared depending on the weather.

•

Do or don't do.

•

The problem is always partly the times—*their times*, of course, *not ours*. Point your first finger into the air. Now let it slowly descend like a tollgate onto the page—

This little hand-drawn picture of a hand, called a manicule, appears frequently in the margins of Renaissance texts. Readers drew this symbol when they wanted to mark a passage; the pointing finger, which functions more or less like a Post-it Note, means something like: THIS. Renaissance readers were trained to collect quotable sayings and to preserve these sayings in commonplace books. They often drew a hand to mark the flowers of rhetoric that they found. In sending Sidney a copy of a letter by the Italian humanist Pietro Bizzarri, Languet suggests that Sidney may want to "cull some flowers" as ornaments for later use, which Sidney then does—and which readers *of* Sidney later did for generations, treating his work as a compendium of rhetorical examples, the ultimate bouquet.

Even if such flowers of rhetoric could eventually be put to some practical purpose, the meaning of the pointing finger that's drawn in the text is perhaps different from the rusted Amcrican billboard that's in the shape of a pointing finger. The billboard clearly signals GO THERE, but the pointing finger sketched in the page margin might elicit a few different translations:

STAY HERE *or*

SEE *or*

WHOA *or*

HOW DELIGHTFUL *or*

HOW FRAGRANT *or*

SMELL

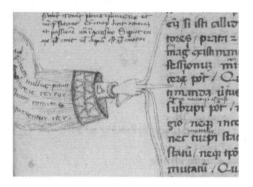

•

Confronted with the perpetual tension in rhetoric between words and things, Erasmus points out the possible self-delusion involved in too great an emphasis on the latter: "We often find," he writes in 1511, "that no one is so apt to lose himself in verbal arguments as the man who boasts that facts, not words, are the only things that interest him." We modern readers have no truck with this argument. We favor the *thing* side of things: we call a spade a spade and know aestheticism when we see it in the road. The play's no longer the thing, insists one critic, "the *thing*'s the thing." The *Arcadia* is for this reason hard on us.

Woolf describes reading Sidney's ornate pages in terms of this same tension: "Words in themselves delight him. Look, he seems to cry, as he picks up the glittering handfuls, can it be true that there are such numbers of beautiful words lying about for the asking? Why not use them, lavishly and abundantly? And so he luxuriates." His prose may sometimes be "absurd," but it is nonetheless the case, Woolf goes on, that "there is a world of difference between writing like this with zest and wonder at the images that form upon one's pen and the writing of later ages when the dew was off the language." Her account of the experience of reading Sidney is remarkably like the experience of reading her description of reading Sidney, with her lavish verbal flourishes and mixed metaphors. Eventually, the style of the book becomes too much; weighed down by its own gildedness, the *Arcadia* begins to sink. She continues: "We have come to long for some plain statement, and the decoration of the style, at first so enchanting, has dulled and decayed.... So by degrees the book floats away into the thin air of limbo. It becomes one of those half-forgotten and deserted places where the grasses grow over fallen statues and the rain drips and the marble steps are green with moss and vast weeds flourish in the flower-beds. And yet it is a beautiful garden to wander in now and then; one stumbles over lovely broken faces, and here and there a flower blooms and the nightingale sings in the lilac-tree." The lavish garden has become a no less lavish graveyard. Notice the flower she makes bloom among the mossy ruins.

•

"Now you see, sir, how your fooling grows old and people dislike it" (*Twelfth Night*, I.5.111–12).

•

It has been suggested that literary genres can be associated with basic bodily processes:

    tragedy—death
    comedy—sex
    satire—defecation

And pastoral romance? surely—napping.

•

The *Arcadia* is a pastoral romance, which means that its adventures unfold in a mythic and idealized landscape far from the realities of rapid urbanization in late sixteenth-century London. Of course, London was not yet the industrialized, overcrowded, crabbed city that Charles Dickens will describe, but buildings were going up, and people were moving in, and London's capitalist roots were pressing down thirstily into the banks of the Thames. Partly because of the discovery of the New World, London's location had in effect shifted: from the remote outskirts of continental Europe, it now stood at the center of a network of highly profitable trade routes that stretched thousands of miles to the West and to the East. The power of merchants rose rapidly, and overspending aristocrats sold off their family estates to raise money. The farmlands surrounding these estates were converted into places of profitable production for wool, England's major export. Thrown off the land, deracinated farm laborers—reeking, in Shakespeare's words, with the "breath of garlic-eaters"—moved to the city and looked for work. Sewage increasingly became a problem. Despising the cautious shopkeepers and traders and "apron-men" to whom they had sold their estates, many aristocrats grew nostalgic. So, too, did many merchants—for lives that had never been theirs. If humanism was always partly a fantasy, characterized by desire for a lost world, this fantasy was one that belonged both to the aristocracy and to the middle classes.

•

The desire that lyric poetry expresses to be free of social realities is itself reflective of those realities, says Adorno: "It implies a protest against a social situation that every individual experiences as hostile, alien, cold, oppressive, and this situation is imprinted in reverse on the poetic work: the more heavily the situation weighs upon it, the more firmly the work resists it by refusing to submit to anything heteronomous and constituting itself solely in accordance with its own laws. The work's distance from mere existence becomes the measure of what is false and bad in the latter."

This negation of reality characterizes pastoral and has done so since the beginning of the genre. Ovid's description of the Golden Age, one of the genre's early precursors, is imprinted with negations: "This was the Golden Age that, without coercion, without laws, spontaneously nurtured the good and the true. There was no fear or punishment; there were no threatening words to be read, fixed in bronze, no crowd of suppliants fearing the judge's face: they lived safely without protection. No pine tree felled in the mountains had yet reached the flowing waves to travel to other lands: human beings knew only their own shores. There were no steep ditches surrounding towns, no straight war-trumpets, no coiled horns, no swords and helmets."

The Golden Age is not knowable in its own right; rather, that mythical age is the inverse of all that is unlikable now. It is not this bad thing; it is not that other bad thing.

With the discovery of the New World, such fantasies found a new home—not in the projections onto a past age, but onto a distant place, seemingly uncorrupted, pure, and virginal. In the late sixteenth century, Michel de Montaigne drew on Ovid in representing the cannibals of Brazil. Notice the similarity of his description: "This is a nation . . . in which there is no sort of traffic, no knowledge of letters, no science of numbers, no name for a magistrate or for political superiority, no custom of servitude, no riches or poverty, no contracts, no successions, no partitions, no occupations but leisure ones, no care for any but common kinship, no clothes, no agriculture, no metal, no use of wine or wheat. The very words that signify lying, treachery, dissimulation, avarice, envy, belittling, pardon—unheard of."

Later, in America, this fantasy was perhaps projected onto the never-never land of the *future*: remember Jack Frost's palace in Little Nemo's Slumberland, which its creator, Winsor McCay, had based partly on the white palaces of the 1893 Chicago World's Fair. Underlying the idealized world of Sidney's *Arcadia* is this impulse to negate the sordidness, sadness, rejection of reality: this landscape is where historical reality isn't. In Slumberland, the name of the boy-hero, Nemo, is Latin and means "no one."

It is a name not unlike Utopia, which means "no place."

But—*soft, soft*—in the land of dreams, one ill-spoken phrase can ruin everything. To realize you are sleeping is to begin to wake up. Nemo must not think about the last two words of that sentence and must not look at Flip's top hat.

•

On June 14, 1940, the day the Germans entered Paris, Virginia Woolf, Vita Sackville-West, and Leonard Woolf took a day trip to Penshurst, where they had a picnic. The Sidney family estate was in the Sevenoaks district of Kent, not far from Vita Sackville-West's family estate, Knole House, which Queen Elizabeth had given in 1561 to Robert Dudley. This estate eventually passed, in 1566, to Vita's ancestor Thomas Sackville, the coauthor of *Gorboduc*, the first English play in blank verse. Virginia Woolf had imagined this house as a kind of symbol of English literary history in her 1928 *Orlando*. As the Nazis marched up the Champs Élysées, the party drove to Penshurst, where, like any other group of tourists, they paid their fee for admission and toured the grounds. As they were leaving, the butler approached them to say that Lord de L'Isle, a descendant of Sir Philip Sidney, would like to see them. The party followed the butler into Lord de L'Isle's private rooms. Virginia Woolf described the day in her diary:

> Paris is in the hands of the Germans. Battle continues. We spent the day seeing Penshurst with Vita—picnicked in the park. Gwen in military dress—V. in trousers. Very fine & hot. The house of yellowish Oxford stone. Banqueting hall: disappointing furniture, like heavy & over ornamental Tot Court Rd. only

made 1314—Q. Elizth dancing—tilted up by Essex? Ladies &
gents all sitting on the benches laughing. Elizabeth herself in
another picture, delicate skinned red haired, aquiline. Then the
shell of Lady Pembroke's lute—like half a fig. Then Sidney's
shaving glass. Then some very ugly tables...a long panelled
room with soft veined panels. Out into the garden, which has
certain trim lawns, & long grass walks, then lapses into wilder-
ness. Sidneys very poor—given up weeding. A great lily pond;
the goldfish making an odd subacqueous tapping as they moved
among reeds. Then through old pink courtyards, with the Boar
& the broad arrow to the car: but the butler came & said his
Lordship wanted to see us. Vita went—we stayed. Then were
summoned. Ld. de Lisle & Dudley is like a very old liver & white
Sussex spaniel—heavy pouched, both eyes with cataract, 87 but
looks younger, waistcoat undone. Glad of company. Easy going
at his ease, loose limbed, twinkling. "Do you mind if I say it—
but the statue of the Q. outside Buck Palace is like a lady on a
close stool—Showed that (Q. Charlotte) to Queen Mary. She
didnt like it when I said it was like her." Padded us into a small
room; made us look at pictures said to be good—one, skied, of
A. Sidney. Then a reputed Rembrandt. Can only keep a few
rooms open. And those like seaside lodging rooms—There we
left him alone, blind, with his shilling box of cork tipped ciga-
rettes, some patience or other game, a few novels, & the pho-

tographs of his nephew "—a very nice boy" & his grey lady the only signs of youth, on a side table. Vita said he'd told her he was so poor he couldnt have people to stay: whole place run by 2 maids & a boy & butler; is alone—but d'you mind being alone? she asked. "Hate it" he said. Twice a week he goes to Tonbridge & plays Bridge. There this old snail sits in the corner of his tremendous shell.

Another record also exists of this day. In the last book of his five-volume autobiography, Leonard Woolf—whose family was Jewish—also describes this visit:

There was something historically absurd and touching, ironically incongruous and yet, in that particular moment of history, appropriate in the spectacle of Vita and Lord de L'Isle and Virginia and me sitting together in that ugly little room.... [Vita's] ancestor, Thomas Sackville, Lord Buckhurst and Earl of Dorset, Lord High Treasurer of England, might well have driven over from Knole to visit Lord de L'Isle's ancestor, Sir Philip Sidney, at Penshurst four hundred years ago. He would not have taken either Virginia's or my ancestors with him, for Virginia's ancestors were laboring as little better than serfs in Aberdeenshire and mine were living "despised and rejected" in some continental ghetto . . . In 1940 the descendants of the Scottish serf and the ghetto Jew, on payment of 2s. 6d. each, visited the banqueting hall and the sitting-rooms and bedrooms . . . while Lord de L'Isle, the owner, and the descendant of Thomas Sackville, sat in a poky little room

drinking tea from rather dreary china. I felt that in that room history had fallen about the ears of the Sidneys and the Leicesters, the Sackvilles and the Dorsets, while outside, across the Channel, in France, history was falling about the ears of us all.

Europe was falling, but this great house had already become a ruin. It was as though history had broken into the fantasy house of literature, into the fantasy of aristocracy, into what has been called *the beautiful lie*. Grass and moss now grew among the furniture, in the bookcases, through the fingers of Lord de L'Isle's hand, which was holding the cigarette and resting on the arm of that ugly "heavy & over ornamental" chair. With his "heavy pouched" eyes, Sir Philip Sidney's descendant liked nothing better than to get away from all that old yellowish Oxford stone and, twice a week, play bridge in Tonbridge.

•

ITEM: *Corot's red hat.*

DEFINITION: A phrase that refers to an aesthetic technique whereby artists introduce into their work a foreign element that breaks the rules established in the rest of this work. The term, which a painter taught me, derives from Corot's practice of adding into a landscape a small spot of bright red, which he uses to represent a hat or scarf or cloak, but which does not otherwise belong to the palette that determines the rest of the painting. To see for yourself the importance of this red spot, all you have to do is cover your view of the hat with your finger. Without this mark, does not the painting become something other than a painting?—a foggy atmosphere, a piece of thick woolen fabric, a scrap of wallpaper, mold on wet twigs, pea soup, some forgotten vegetable in the back of the refrigerator's bottom drawer?

If we broaden the application of this technique to the literary arts, we might observe a version of Corot's red hat at work in the plays of Shakespeare. It is commonly said that he creates plays of mixed genres. Polonius in *Hamlet* could be describing Shakespeare's own work: "tragedy, comedy, history, pastoral, pastorical-comical-historical-pastoral, tragical-historical, tragical-comical-historical-pastoral." What this also means is that Shakespeare routinely triggers various genre expectations and then breaks these expectations. For example, in act IV of his late romance *The Winter's Tale*, he establishes the genre of pastoral, bringing onstage country people crowned with flowers who dance and sing, but he also introduces into this idealized, literary, antihistorical world a character called Autolycus. Autolycus, who is constantly trying to pawn off his "trumpery," does not come from the world of idealized pastoral literature, but rather from the contemporary world of London: he is a city rogue. He comes from (among other places) late sixteenth-century pamphlets, specifically Robert Greene's *Cony-Catcher* pamphlets, which describe the venality of "real" London life with its pickpockets and swindlers and con men:

But gentlemen, these cony-catchers, these vultures, these fatal Harpies, that putrify with their infections this flourishing estate of England, as if they had their consciences sealed with a hot iron, & that as men delivered up into a reprobate sense, grace were utterly exiled from their hearts, so with the deaf adder they not only stop their ears against the voice of the charmer, but dissolutely without any spark of remorse stand upon their bravadoes, and openly in words & actions maintain their palpable and manifest cozenages, swearing by no less than their enemy's blood, even by God himself, that they will make a massacre of his bones, and cut off my right hand for penning down their abominable practices: but alas for the poor snakes, words are wind, & looks but glances: every thunderclap hath not a bolt, nor every cony-catcher's oath an execution. I live still, & I live to display their villainies, which, gentlemen you shall see set down in most ample manner in this small treatise.

In the world of pastoral, Autolycus ventriloquizes the voice of these rogues, as well as the style of the narrator who supposedly exposes them, and in so doing functions as a kind of red hat in that he breaks the genre—popping us out of the world of ostensibly time-less art and into the world of sixteenth- and seventeenth-century London, the realm of our reality, which is the very thing that the characters discuss when Autolycus tries to sell them a ballad that will, he claims, tell of the latest news and the most recent wonders, such as of a woman on the coast who was turned into a fish on Wednesday, the fourscore of April: "Is it true, think you?" asks Mopsa. "Very true," he answers. "Pray now, buy some," she urges. "I love a ballad in print, a-life, for then we are sure they are *true*."

Shakespeare seems modern when he makes this move—and he makes it a lot. He seems modern because at such moments he appears to be pulling us out of the realm of art and pushing us into the realm of *reality* (even if that reality is also itself a fiction). It's as though he establishes a frame and then creates a figure that breaks that frame—so that we feel he has stepped into actuality.

However—*if I could just have your attention for a minute more*—not all artists want this effect. There are some artists who actually want their readers to remain within the artful world of the text—and they resist ever breaking the aesthetic terms they

establish. In the realm of the visual arts, many Renaissance tapestries are hard for us to see because all their elements seem to be of one kind. We moderns experience a sudden sense of visual confusion; we cannot distinguish figure from ground; the parts of the work blend together into one thing; this thing seems removed from us; we walk to another part of the gallery, or to the cafeteria. Yet what would it be to try to enter such a world? To try, provisionally, to accept its terms, in their *emphatic artificiality*, and to exist for a moment in a realm that does not want to seem real? We will need to stand still for a moment; to allow our eyes to adjust; to pause ... and do you see what happens? the figures will have started to move ...

Sidney's work is of this kind. The hats in his *Arcadia* are never red, and they never have words written on them telling you to wake up.

—But the time! Excuse me.

•

The *Arcadia* begins: "It was in the time that the earth begins to put on her new apparel...." In Arcadia, everything is clothed; everything is ornamented. The fruit are golden jewels that hang from the earlobes of the trees; the branches are ribbons that float in the wind; &c.; &c. Even nakedness, when it is especially handsome, appears to be a kind of clothing. Sidney describes his hero, Musidorus, who washes up naked on the shore of the book's opening few pages: "Though he were naked, nakedness was to him an apparel." The rhetoric itself is clothed and covered with ornaments.

In the portraits of sixteenth-century aristocrats, a lust for intricacy and ornament shows immediately in the clothing. *Elaborate* is a late sixteenth-century word: "produced or accomplished by labor." The ornate detail of the clothing makes the faces, by contrast, appear plain and smooth. Like the face of God that hovers over medieval maps, the faces in the portraits float over vast landscapes of intricately embroidered detail. Each inch of their clothing might represent four months of a man's or woman's life.

"They are the lords and owners of their faces," says Shakespeare of the cool and cruel aristocrats (sonnet 94). Not only are they the lords and owners of their faces, but also, we might feel as we stroll through the gallery and peer at the tiny pearls sewn into their ermine-lined doublets, they are the lords and owners of all the pricked fingers and strained eyes of seamstresses and furriers and weavers in London, Bruges, and Arras. Montaigne describes the visit of three native people from Brazil to the court of the child-king Charles IX and his bearded entourage of Swiss guards in Rouen: the Brazilians, he reports, "were shown our ways, our splendor, the aspect of a fine city. After that, someone asked their opinion, and wanted to know what they had found most amazing." Montaigne recalls that the Brazilians said, first, that "they thought it very strange that so many grown men, bearded, strong, and armed . . . should submit to obey a child, and that one of them was not chosen to command instead." And, second, no less odd, was that "there were among us men full and gorged with all sorts of good things," while others were "beggars at their doors, emaciated with hunger and poverty." Why did these half-starved crowds "endure such an injustice"? Why did they not "take the others by the throat, or set fire to their houses"? To the native Brazilians, new to the ways of Europe, it was difficult to understand why a child-king should rule when there were nearby healthy adults, and why some people should be well housed and well fed when multitudes were homeless and scrounging for scraps. When reflected in the mirrors of these Brazilians' eyes, how strange the aristocrats' faces start to appear, looking out at us from over those collars. Their faces have the beguiling placidity of generals who, from the height of their horses, will in a moment initiate, with a flick of their hand, the death of tens of thousands of soldiers and civilians. Under what conditions is placidity an inverse image of other people's anguish?

•

Failed Arcadia 1

The Verrazzano-Narrows Bridge, which connects Staten Island to Brooklyn, is named after Giovanni da Verrazzano, a Florentine who in 1524 was the first European since the Vikings to explore and describe the northeast coast of America, including the harbor of New York, where I now live. He had been commissioned by the French to look for a western route to China. Verrazzano reached America near Cape Fear and traveled along the coast. When he and his men got off the boat to explore the natural riches that this new land had to offer, they encountered a small group of native people cowering in the grass. The Europeans decided to take some of them back to France. As he describes in a letter to King François I, they kidnapped a little boy and tried to take a young woman, who was, according to Verrazzano, "very beautiful and tall." But she resisted. The explorers offered her food, which she threw angrily to the ground. When they tried to seize her, she screamed so loudly and unrelentingly that they found it impossible to carry her all the way to their ships, which were two leagues away, and had to leave her behind. That was how this sixteenth-century native woman avoided the brutalities awaiting her aboard ship. Examining an early scribal copy of this letter, preserved at the Morgan Library in New York, I see where

Verrazzano has placidly added on the next page this marginal note in what is believed to be his own hand:

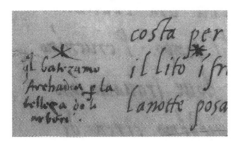

...*quale batezamo Archadia per la bellaza de li arbori.*
...which we baptized Arcadia on account of the beauty of the trees.

The name *Arcadia* was picked up by later cartographers. It can be found on maps beginning in 1548 and, after morphing into *L'Acadie*, it migrated north and became the French name for what is now Nova Scotia.

•

Montaigne posits this challenge: Ask a man at dinner for his most cherished philosophy of life, and you will find that it's not worth the soup. "There is nothing so insipid in all the dishes on your table as this fine entertainment of his mind," he writes. Behind the much-discussed "Renaissance discovery of the greatness of man" lived just such an understanding, at heart religious, that pulsed constantly in the veins of both Protestants and Catholics of the period: the wisdom of man is vanity, vanity, vanity. Here, for example, is Katherine Parr, the sixth and final wife of Henry VIII, in 1544 mortifying herself in translating the fifth psalm: "Yea, I am a very babe and a child, and know full little mine own life and conversation. My lips be defiled and unclean; my time is short, and I am not able to understand Thy law."

Further reading: Paul's first epistle to the Corinthians, Erasmus's *In Praise of Folly*, the fool in *King Lear*.

•

There may be literary works where the professed ideas represent a relatively superficial level of the text's overall meaning. The Austrian Jewish literary historian and philologist Leo Spitzer, who emigrated from Nazi Germany to Turkey to the US, where he took a position at Johns Hopkins University in Baltimore, centers his analysis of Rabelais's work not on the level of its consciously expressed claims—but

rather on the peculiarities of its style. He focuses, for example, on Rabelais's neologisms like *pantagruélisme*, which offers the strange combination of a fanciful name (*"pantagruél"*) and a learned philosophical suffix (*"isme"*). Spitzer uses this superficial aspect of Rabelais's language to trace his way to the inner core and unconscious life of this text: Rabelais, he says, "creates word-families, representative of gruesome fantasy-beings, copulating and engendering before our eyes, which have reality only in the world of language, which are established in an intermediate world between reality and irreality, between the nowhere that frightens and the 'here' that reassures." Such peculiarities of style can be like magic doors that, as we run our hands over the text, surprise us by suddenly flying open and allowing us into a secret inner chamber.

In the case of Sidney's *Arcadia*, one such peculiarity of style lies in his intricate sentence structures, which depend on a series of balanced clauses. To a modern ear, these sentences may sound overly ornate, trinketish. They may even vaguely offend us— *vaguely* because, when asked, we will not know why *any* literary style could possibly offend us (with the assumption being, who could really care?). But, still, the sentences jingle. To change metaphors: their little wings flutter at our eardrums. They seem overly worked, too clever, mannered, foppish, affected, precious, decadent, effete, unmanly, flowery, sissy, artificial, contrived, too studied, la-di-da, you know, flickety-flick. They're—(here a gesture of the hand that's like a little bird that struggles to escape the clutches of a ravenous animal and that, suddenly wrenching free from its jaws, flies away).

(The diligent notetaker pauses uncertainly; the pen lifts and hovers over the page—.)

•

A brief history of prose style:

At the turn of the seventeenth century, a major shift can be observed in the prose style of many leading English writers: what emerges in the modern era is a kind of prose that is plainer, more irregular, more infused with colloquial rhythms and phrases, more like *realistic* speech. Ben Jonson typifies this development: if he sets up a parallelism in the beginning of a sentence, he will break it by the end. The effect is that the *real* language of the city has broken in.

What went *out* of fashion—which is what concerns us—is what the Princeton historian of style Morris William Croll calls an "oratorical style." (In a biographical note included in his posthumous collection of essays, we learn that Professor Croll, who was born in 1872 in Gettysburg, Pennsylvania, never married, lived with his sister Elsie at 40 Bayard Lane, and had a "soft and precise enunciation, with an occasional sibilant emphasis just rising above a whisper.") This oratorical style—which may be the oldest style of which there is a theory that could be taught—was characterized by *schemata verborum*, which Morris described as "similarities or repetitions of sound used as purely sensuous devices to give pleasure or aid the attention." In other words, this is a style that was meant to appeal to the ear. Its ancient models include speeches by sophists like Gorgias, whose reputation Socrates has forever ruined. Their aim was not philosophical but aesthetic and, potentially, political: this style was not necessarily intended for the private search for truth, but for the influence of king, court, or assembly. In the era of the Roman Republic, Cicero revived this art. What's important to emphasize about this style, says Croll, is "the sensuous character of its appeal to its audience. Its 'round composition' and the 'even falling of its clauses' do not always satisfy the inward ear of the solitary reader. Heard solely by the reflective mind, it is an empty, a frigid, or an artificial style. But it is not meant for such a hearing. It is addressed first, like music, to the physical ear. . . ." What if Sidney's *Arcadia* were one of the last and lavish descendants of this style from the era of its dominancy—its final hurrah before falling into desuetude?

When we hear this style, we are hearing the distant bellow of a nearly extinct animal.

•

The advocate for the ornate oratorical style rises to his feet. Pausing for a moment, he looks down, and then begins speaking:

"Esteemed court: You think that my client plays with words while your client works with things. You think that the speech of my client is merely aesthetic, while the speech of your client is straightforward, honest, forthright. But let us pause for a moment before giving a veneer of truth to our splendid falsehoods. I do not question that the trappings of rhetoric can lie on my side of the debate, but I challenge whether such trappings cannot also lie on your side. I do not question whether my client could be guilty, but I question whether your client must be innocent.

"Does the ornate necessarily mean the false? Does the simple invariably mean the true? Is it really so easy to determine where the truth lies? And is not the truth precious enough that we should treat the search for it with the utmost care? Gentlemen. Permit me to remind you of the history. As my expert witness Professor Croll has pointed out, the rise of the plain style was in many ways a cynical recognition arising from Machiavellian realpolitik, and from the insight that the most important political decisions were no longer occurring before the assembly in the open public. Rather, such decisions were being worked out privately in politicians' back rooms. Oratory, as Marc-Antoine Muret boldly asserted, was now useless—merely ornamental. A new era was emerging that spoke in the language of what Shakespeare called 'cool reason.' As Professor Croll has just shown, the advocates of the severe style themselves were soon liable to verbal excesses, affecting a tone of solemn majesty and a new kind of pomp. Of this *stile coupé* Professor Croll wrote: 'Each member is as short as the most alert intelligence would have it. The period consists, as some of its admirers were wont to say, of the nerves and muscles of speech alone; it is as hard-bitten, as free of soft or superfluous flesh, as *one of Caesar's soldiers*.'

"The question that emerges for us today is whether the supposedly plain portrayal of things 'as they really are' conceals (maybe even from itself) the seductive role of words, leaving us vulnerable to increasingly crude verbal manipulations. How can we, as moderns, believe in all seriousness that the *genus humile* is the language of truth after we have heard our own politicians desperately trying to manipulate the public into believing through their plain talk that they are just regular folks who love hot dogs, children, SUVs, God, and the great outdoors like anyone else? Our politicians humble-mumble from one side of their mouths, 'This foreign policy stuff is a little frustrating' (George W. Bush, *New York Daily News*, April 23, 2002), while deftly rearranging the balance of global power to benefit themselves and their friends from the other side of their mouths. But times are quickly getting harder and ever more bald and brutal, and even doublespeak is now starting to seem almost too literary. 'I don't care,' says Donald Trump, 'I'm really rich' (announcement of his presidential campaign, June 16, 2015). Are not the ornate and plain styles, in the end, both forms of rhetoric, both having the capacity to seduce and to trick? Does one style necessarily possess the claim on truth and morality—or, rather, do we have to put our preconceptions to one side and evaluate both kinds of speech on a case-by-case basis on their own terms? I assert to you today that it is only through attention to words that we can hope to become less naively susceptible to the seductions of words—which is what teachers of rhetoric since Aristotle have claimed. When this awareness of words is gone, we are led like sheep.

"Your Honors, let us not wander from one error to another. I beg you to take my client on his own terms—and listen to the perceptions, even the insights, that he, even he, in his elaborate style, may offer.

"I have nothing further."

•

In the sixteenth century, some words were valued for being outlandish. Here is George Puttenham's 1589 definition of a rhetorical figure called the "Far-fetched": "But the sense is much altered and the hearer's conceit strangely entangled by the figure *meta-*

lepsis, which I call the Far-fetched. As when we had rather fetch a word a great way off than to use one nearer hand to express the matter as well and plainer."

•

And yet, there emerge arguments on the other side of the question. I hear about a man who was leaving his wife and children, leaving them in poverty. He said, "It has become necessary for us to separate and for me to pursue a new course, fulfilling my potential (or attempting to) through a relationship with ——." But his wife expressed a different sense of language, one less Latinate and less abstract: "*Asshole*," she said, and she punctuated that word in the most concrete way possible, by throwing a vase against the wall near his head. Thus, the plain style has its moments, too, and on key occasions restores language when it has wandered woefully off course.

•

For some of us—especially those who grew up poor, or maybe middle class, or in some ways one and in some ways the other, or who lived in inner cities, or perhaps rural areas, or who grew up in America, or let's say overseas, or maybe who were just born in

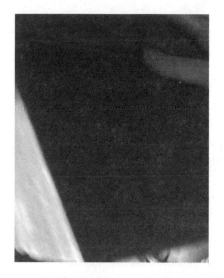

the twentieth or twenty-first century—reading or any other form of intellectual life was a covert operation, a secret act that we did not admit to in public. For me, in public might mean on the low wall in front of our apartment building in Washington, DC, or in the neighborhood park, or at the local laundromat. In these places, we had to stay alert, ready to outmaneuver our opponents, which is to say, all people other than ourselves. Sometimes verbal finesse did the trick, but at other times more extreme measures were required. For example, my best friend taught me the principle of sudden escalation: If you find yourself in a situation where you are the weaker party, or are outnumbered, and it is clear that you are about to be beaten up, or raped, or both, you must act quickly. In general, pleading does not work, for that only reassures your opponent that you are indeed the chickenshit that you appear to be. Rather, against all expectations to the contrary, it is incumbent upon you to heighten drastically the violence anticipated in the encounter—and to do so suddenly and without any hesitation. The logic is simple: your apparent irrationality will establish a new ground of power. *"Look at his eyes! That boy is totally crazy!"* said one of the young men who had only begun to warm to the task of beating up my best friend when, without warning, this friend (a skinny, somewhat effeminate-looking boy of great courage) had spun around screeching like a feral animal, with a broken bottle gripped in his hand. Even squirrels, remember, are scary when they are crazed. In response to such situations, we might pose the following question: How do the pressures of the present shape the contours of our inner life? The need to maintain a state of readiness for apparent insanity, or for lying, or irony, or flirtation, or intimidation, or for playing the fool (and playing the fool so long and so well that we may convince even ourselves that we are a fool) keeps us out of our dream worlds but also, perhaps, creates the space for them—even when our only awareness of such worlds is of where we are forbidden to go. What would a literary criticism look like that could somehow take cognizance of such conditions of mental life?

•

Among the oldest ancestors of the European pastoral paradise are the ancient bucolic songs found in Theocritus's *Idylls* and

Virgil's *Eclogues*, songs sung by shepherds amid their grazing flocks. There is also the related tradition of the *locus amoenus* (pleasant place), where heroes like Odysseus, stranded on lovely Kalypso's isle, are tempted to abandon their bright quests in favor of the shade of sensual pleasures. In the Renaissance, Torquato Tasso

shows his hero Rinaldo, having lost all awareness of his quest, lounging in the lap of the enchantress Armida, on an island where everything appears as soft and sweet and ripe as fruit. Rinaldo looks into her eyes, where he sees a reflection of himself looking into her eyes—the image of self-indulgent pleasure. His friends only manage to rouse him from his sensual and dreamy state by holding up a mirrored shield that shows Rinaldo the truth of himself—i.e., what a Pussy he's become. Only then, confronted by his own image, does our hero reawaken to his manly quest and abandon the island.

In Spenser's *Faerie Queene*, the hero's reaction against this sensual paradise is even more severe. Guyon, the Knight of Temperance, utterly destroys the Bower of Bliss:

But all those pleasant bowers and palace brave,
Guyon broke down, with rigor pitiless;
Ne ought their goodly workmanship might save
Them from the tempest of his wrathfulness,
But that their bliss he turned to balefulness:
Their groves he felled, their gardens did deface,
Their arbors spoiled, their cabinets suppress,
Their banquet houses burn, their buildings raze,
And of the fairest late, now made the foulest place.

For a knight of temperance, Guyon's reaction is peculiarly extreme: consider his "rigor pitiless" and "the tempest of his wrathfulness." Why not just leave this bower, as heroes in other epics have done? Why deface, spoil, suppress, burn, raze it? This scene follows one where Guyon is tempted to join two seductresses playing in a fountain, and readers have long noticed the quality of self-repression in this passage. It has been said that wine comes out more forcefully from narrow-necked bottles, and Guyon perhaps enacts the violence that emerges from self-aggression. The need is to destroy the object that offers the bliss that Guyon cannot allow himself. (Note that Spenser does not call the garden a bower of *false* bliss.)

Adorno and Horkheimer would consider this the violence of Western civilization, which entails not only violence against nature and the "other," but also violence against the self. Born into a legacy of self-renunciation, the seemingly reasonable man refuses his own creaturely pleasures for aggressive productivity—an exchange that can only occur through a kind of self-brutality. Violence against the other and the self are, seen through this lens, inextricable.

And one might add to this analysis a further level: that *reading* itself represents a kind of *locus amoenus*. It is a pleasure that occurs in the soft bower of our studies or bedrooms. In those passages where aggression is directed against the bower, is the text also not turning with hostility against itself—?

•

Failed Arcadia 2

Vivian Gordon Harsh, born in 1890, was the first African American head librarian in the Chicago Public Library system, at the George Cleveland Hall Branch on Chicago's South Side, where she helped build a national collection devoted to black literature and history. This collection was fundamental to the emergence of the Chicago Black Renaissance. Visitors to the library included Richard Wright and Langston Hughes. In time, a neighborhood spot was named in her honor, the Vivian Gordon Harsh Park. It was in this park one afternoon eight years ago that Hadiya Pendleton, fifteen years old, was talking with her friends when rain clouds unexpectedly rolled in, as they sometimes do in Chicago near the lake. The group sought shelter under a canopy near some swings. Suddenly, one of her friends noticed a man jumping over the park fence and running toward them. *The New York Times* of January 31, 2013, reports:

> He ran toward the group and started shooting, then jumped into a vehicle, which drove away, according to the police.
>
> "It is believed that the offender mistook the group for gang members and fired at them," said Joshua Purkiss, an officer with the Chicago Police Department.
>
> Another boy was shot once in the leg, but is in good condition. A third victim had a graze wound.
>
> Ms. Jones said a friend cradled Ms. Pendleton's head in her lap as they waited for the ambulance. Ms. Jones held her hand. They thought she would pull through.

Hadiya Pendleton had been a majorette and loved Latin. After her death, her Latin teacher wrote that it had been a privilege to instruct Pendleton, and that she was "a solid citizen in our Latin Republic." He complained that Supreme Court Justice Antonin Scalia's pro-gun majority opinion was based on a misinterpretation of the basic grammar of the Second Amendment. The first clause about "a well regulated militia" is not purposive, as Scalia had claimed; rather, it is closer to an ablative absolute, which "establishes context for the core right, not purpose." Therefore, the question should be what constitutes proper regulation. This high school teacher noted that Pendleton had chosen to be known in the class as *Civis Pretiosior*, the "More Precious Citizen." He closed his essay: "This semester, grief will lend *gravitas* to our study."

•

Et in Arcadia ego, even in Arcadia am I. It is generally understood that death is the speaker. Thus: I (that is, Death) can be found even in Arcadia. Consider Nicolas Poussin's rendition, where a group of young people discover this saying inscribed on a tomb. Note the old man in the lower right, a river god or perhaps Father Time, who seems not to find anything new in this unexpected reminder of death, nothing he did not already know. He has turned away and, as the young people decipher the in-

scription, busies himself with his water jug. The picture can be read from left to right: the moment before the awareness of death (the young shepherds), death itself (the tomb inscription), and then the self-aware acceptance of death (the old man). The sky behind the figures is so eerie and so mysterious in the moment before darkness descends that the very experience of ephemerality becomes beautiful and almost compensatory for death. Poussin was thirty-three years old when he painted this picture; he had arrived in Rome a few years before. The tomb evokes not only his or the viewer's own lost youth, but also perhaps the lost youth of history, as suggested by the ruins of classical antiquity that were then everywhere in Rome; the ephemerality is personal and historical at the same time. Cultures die, too, you know.

In the late 1630s, about a dozen years later, Poussin painted another version of this scene. The sky seems to have stabilized, as has the composition. Poussin has arranged the figures in a central triangle, reinforced by the leaning tree trunk in the background. The ephemerality has given way to a new kind of composure and quality of permanence. Most interesting, note what

has happened to the pointing fingers, especially the pointing finger of the central figure with the beard. He seems to be drawing the edge of his own shadow. According to Pliny, this is the way painting began. While some say that painting began in Egypt, others in Sicyon, others in Corinth, "all agree that it began with tracing an outline round a man's shadow." Thus, Poussin has brought together two pivotal moments: the discovery of death and the discovery of painting. What do these two discoveries have to do with each other? Does art emerge as a response to the encounter with the fact of death? The idyllic landscape of Arcadia is a dream, an escape from death, but, as in a dream, one encounters what is disturbing about reality even there.

•

AND: now the pastoral genre itself is dead. Words like *reed pipe*, *flock*, *sycamore*, *shade* no longer have the capacity to touch our hearts—at least not without an effort of our imaginations. The words are so dead that they don't even have the capacity to make us think about death. It is as though the genre has nothing to do with our own personal or collective histories or wellsprings of feeling. It is hard even to believe that the genre could have once touched the wounds of other people's intimate experiences or made them feel the sweetness of their most painful longings or griefs.

YET: The genre is somehow not dead enough so as to evoke our awe and reverence or to lay claim to the dignity that is reserved for what is ancient. Pastoral is not yet so old that we expect it to demand our respect. In contrast, a museum room with an Egyptian mummy, say, or a fragment of papyrus, has the dignity of a senate hall; the air becomes thicker around those glass cases. All we have to do is to read the dates aloud to each other, and it will seem as if we have said something meaningful. Our companions will gratify us by responding in a hushed breath, "*Amazing.*"

SO: Perhaps pastoral resides in some in-between zone of the culturally dead—so dead that the genre feels distant, yet not dead enough to have become a monument to time. Among dead genres, pastoral is the unlamented and unburied. However, if unburied ghosts wail as their souls flit around the shores of the underworld, the ghosts of dead shepherds have it harder. If they visit us at all, these once-handsome shepherds, their shades smell of mothballs. They appear on embroidered pillows, potpourri dispensers, or other tchotchkes, and produce an effect of melancholy and stale air.

•

But it's also that the pastoral is an emphatically literary genre and we live in an emphatically literal-minded age. Pastoral is the dream-space of literature. Its nature is not natural. Its love is not possible. Its shepherds know nothing about manure, or the sale of wool, or the pH balance of soil. The degree to which our age is literal can be measured by the degree to which the genre of pastoral makes no sense to us, leaves us cold. What would it mean to start to hear the space of pastoral as a kind of echo chamber where our own distance from the world of dream could be sounded?

Adorno says, "The literal is barbaric." If that is so, we are barbaric—very barbaric.

•

Only occasionally, after everyone had left, when in the privacy of your room you used to read a book you really loved, were you aware of your limbs, one leg resting against another, one foot burrowing under another, all the pairs of your symmetrical being sleeping peacefully, as the ark of your young self drifted out… in search of…

•

Never are you fully present to yourself, suggests Augustine in the *Confessions*. He points out that the chambers of memory are vaster and hold more than you can know. How is it possible, he asks, that the extent of yourself exceeds yourself? It must be that God contains you, since you cannot contain yourself.

This is where a religious understanding intersects with a psychoanalytic one. Augustine does not contain himself because his conscious mind is part of something vastly larger—whether that something larger is the unconscious mind or God, he or He. Borges says that the "subliminal self" is surely a less beautiful notion than a god or a muse, but "we have to put up with the mythology of our time." For Borges, both the subliminal self and the muse are metaphors—but for what?

•

There was once a monk named Sarapion. He resided with his brothers in the desert of Scetis, in remote Egypt, around the turn of the fifth century. News came to these brothers of a new doctrine: according to Patriarch Theophilus of Alexandria, Christians had taken too literally Genesis 1:26, which claimed that man had been created in the "image and likeness" of God. This passage, the patriarch said, must be understood in a spiritual rather than a literal sense because, surely, God is above all bodies and does not resemble anything human or even anything that can be "apprehended by the eye or seized by the mind." A deacon was tasked with explaining this doctrine to the hermits of Scetis, and he finally succeeded in convincing them. Realizing their terrible error, these pious brothers began to pray together, thanking God for having led them back to the truth. Suddenly, however, the old monk Sarapion burst into tears. Saint John Cassian reports:

> And then amid these prayers the old man became confused, for he sensed that the particular human image of God which he used to draw before him as he prayed was now gone from his heart. Suddenly he gave way to the bitterest, most abundant tears and sobs. He threw himself on the ground and with the mightiest howl he cried out: "Ah the misfortune! They've taken my God away from me, and now I don't have one I might hold on to, and I don't know whom to adore or whom to call out to."

Convinced by the deacon's argument, the poor old monk discovered that the God to which he had devoted his life was, in an instant, no longer in his heart. He had no image to which to turn, at least not one in which he could still believe. And how could he love that which had no image?

This question could be posed: What would it mean to love an image that isn't—in any literal or factual sense—real? For, in defense of Sarapion, wasn't it also the orthodox deacon who was being literal in his objection to Sarapion's imagistic spiritual practice? To object that Sarapion's image of God wasn't literally real

71

is to assert an understanding of truth that is, paradoxically, based in the literal. The iconoclast takes up his axe and hacks at the sculptures in the church—chopping off their heads and hands, almost as though these sculptures were living people who had the power to hurt him. But, *good sir!*, those are only images after all.

•

The need to write in fragments (or, let's say, in *clouds*) is considered a modernist phenomenon, having to do with the fragmentation of experience under conditions of industrialized modern life, but Petrarch also felt this need in the fourteenth century. His *Canzoniere* is a collection of poems that tells its story (to the extent it has a story) through gaps, or, more accurately, through flashes of consciousness that are and are not continuous. Partly the discontinuity results from the narrative blanks between the events described in the various poems (vision of Laura, death of Laura, and so on), but also from the differences in the genres or structures of thought that the poems employ (dream vision, allegory, visual description), differences that endow these structures with a freshly provisional quality and fictionality. The poems build scaffolding around what they describe, and then this scaffolding comes down again.

•

Sturdy and broad-chested even in her early nineties, my grand-mother on my father's side had been an athlete when she was young, a regional champion in tennis and field hockey, and liked to brag that there were still people hobbling around the neigh-borhood whose shins she had broken. Only in her last couple years did she become unsteady on her feet. As she walked down the long hallway of her apartment in Chicago's South Side, she would balance herself with one hand against the wall while her rubbery orthopedic walking shoes would make a slight suctioning sound on the linoleum floor.

Her apartment had no air conditioner because, generous with others, she did not like to spend money on herself—except, that is, to attend the Chicago Opera, taking the #6 bus both ways. In the afternoon, when it was hottest, she kept the shades down. In the morning and evening, she raised them. It was always correct to comment on the breeze from Lake Michigan that filled her curtains, lifting and letting them fall. "The air from the lake is what keeps the place cool," she would happily explain. I rarely left this apartment while I was visiting, so for me the lake was almost imaginary, and there was something magical about her regularly evoking the lake to explain the temperature of the apart-ment, as though my ideas had gotten confused and her apartment was somehow akin to the cool shadowy underwater world of that lake.

In the peak of summer, during the day, she would often read with her polyester shirt half unbuttoned in the front, and her bra—as sturdy and thick as construction site scaffolding—showed a little, but not indecently. Sometimes she would watch television. In the evening, after dinner, she and I used to sit on the back porch with a scotch ("Now, now pour with a generous hand, my love"), and I would read Willa Cather to her, describing the endless fields of grass in the West. I would tilt the book to catch the light from the kitchen window behind me, as my grandmother would look out wistfully over the parking lot.

•

The lobby of the Chicago Lyric Opera, with its ornately gilded decorations and flying cupids, is itself already a kind of theater

 set, already a kind of Swan Castle. As we take our seats, the wild and discordant sounds of the orchestra tuning up seem to evoke, and then to dissipate, the hassle of getting here—the

last-minute searching for the tickets and the house keys, the slamming of doors, and then the jostling ride along Lake Shore Drive on the bus. When the curtains rise, all of that noise and confusion is gone, like a mist that has lifted, and it is as if we are reawakened into a new kind of reality. At first, the darkness limits our view to just the small pools that the spotlight allows us, through which the singers move like beautiful river manatees, enormous but buoyant, as though their bodies are supported by the medium of sound, and then the light gets brighter as the stage fills with soldiers carrying shields and spears. Slowly, we release ourselves into the world of the dream . . . Now here comes one of the great singers, who, when he sings his aria, holds his hands up into the air, with his fingers curled as if he were holding something heavy, the mighty substance perhaps of his feelings, and I glance at my grandmother, who, with her half-closed eyes, appears painfully immersed in his feelings—painfully because she knows what the Knight of the Swan and poor Elsa of Brabant apparently do not—how tragically their love will soon end. *Do not ask me who I am, or where I come from*, the Knight sings to Elsa. *That is the one thing you cannot know. Love me only as you behold me right now*. The plot of *Lohengrin* concerns the conditions of faith, but the plot could also be understood as turning on the refusal of historical knowledge. At the core of the story is the lesson that what has been called spiritual power can tolerate no awareness of history. Such magic draws a circle around itself. Thomas Mann felt, every time he listened to the opera, "like a boy of 18." But even if as children we never heard of *Lohengrin* or of Wagner, the prelude will still seem to recall our childhoods. On the bus ride home, I ask my grandmother how she liked the performance. "My girlish heart was beating like mad," she said, holding her large and muscular fist against her chest to show me what her heart had done.

•

Married briefly at sixteen to the painter George Frederic Watts, the Shakespearean actress Ellen Terry posed also for Julia Mar-

garet Cameron and John Singer Sargent. She was an actress who understood portraits. The photographs of her playing Portia in *The Merchant of Venice*, Cordelia in *King Lear*, Beatrice in *Much Ado about Nothing*, and (in this picture) Hermione in *The Winter's Tale* should be classed among the great translations—from Shakespeare's English into the language of images. She knew how to register in her face and posture the shadow of her character's inner being.

The age of photography was new; what it meant to pose for a portrait was still defined by the age of painting. Terry poses for her photograph as though she were posing for a long time; she is waiting, allowing her character to be known by letting herself be looked at. The image is not about the instant but about duration. If this photograph is in this way unlike later photographs, it is also like them in its underlying condition of pain. A mechanical image promises objectivity, which means that the one posing says, *You see how beautiful I am when you are not here?* This is the self-negating contradiction of intimacy without interaction. A version of this kind of pain exists in the story that Herodotus tells of the king Candaules, who is so in love with his wife that he arranges for his guard Gyges to see how beautiful she is when she is naked. The king's ensuing death—her vengeance for this betrayal—in a sense concretizes the negation he has already inflicted on himself. This is also the pain that exists in *The Winter's Tale*, where Leontes imagines his beloved wife having an affair with his oldest friend—and then is consumed with jealousy for the joys that are in fact already his.

A gap of sixteen years separates the first three acts from the last two in *The Winter's Tale*, and Shakespeare redeems many of the losses the characters have endured. Perdita, the king's abandoned daughter, is found. Hermione, the queen who has been thought dead, turns out to be alive. The statue that looks so amazingly like Hermione is—most wonderfully—actually Hermione. Hermione has preserved herself, she says in that magical moment when she steps off the platform to take her husband's hand and then touch her daughter's head, "to see the issue." But in this play that is all about the fantastical restoration of losses, some losses are never redeemed. Once the young prince Mamillius dies, he is dead, and no magic brings him back.

However, Mamillius does get to experience one restoration during his brief life. This occurs in the beginning of the second act, at the moment just before he tells his story, his winter's tale, directly to his mother in her ear so that no one else can hear it. Weary with a second pregnancy, she had sent him away to play with her women, but then, after a moment, she turns back to the boy and says these magical words: "I am for you again."

•

When Odysseus finally returns home, after twenty years during which his family didn't know whether he was alive or dead, he takes off his disguise to reveal who he really is to his son. But Telemachos at first doesn't believe that this man—with his dark skin, fine clothing, firm jaw, and black beard—can be anyone but a god. Odysseus insists that he is Telemachos's father, the very man for whom Telemachos has been grieving all these years: "No other Odysseus than I will ever come back to you." After all your suffering and enduring and grieving and searching—here I am, a single embodied being.

Time in this moment comes to a trembling point. Telemachos's fantasy of his father meets the actuality of him. Everything for a moment hovers, as though suspended . . . What is so amazing, Telemachos, about this moment? Reality, for once, has something to do with your needs, and you stand astonished.

•

Thought experiment: In a given period, what is the inherent connection between the dominant technology of artistic representation and the dominant worldview? In medieval literature, God's viewpoint is often depicted as one of simultaneity, as the so-called *nunc stans*—or "standing now." In the *Confessions*, for example, Augustine repeatedly contrasts the simultaneity of God with his own painful human existence, stretched out in time. Unlike mortal beings, God does not see reality as it unfolds, but rather perceives all moments at the same time, in a single instant. Plotinus praised the Egyptians for their hieroglyphs, which, unlike the letters of a word that must be read sequentially, can be seen as pictures, all at once, thereby conveying their divine ideas without "discursiveness." Plotinus was trying to provide a way of imagining how the Intellect of God could see all time "with one glance of its mind," as Boethius put it, as if all time were a single image. In medieval paintings, the evident distortions in the depictions of space are not, contrary to popular perception, accidents or failures yet to have attained single-point perspective. Rather, the paintings aspire to this all-encompassing perspective of the *nunc stans* by showing more than one viewpoint at the same time. The platform on which a saint stands resembles a house in a Cézanne landscape because, in both cases, the painter has allowed the viewer to see, impossibly, the front and two sides at the same time—that is, to see simultaneously, as God sees, different views of the object at one time. The medievals were not failing to achieve the "realism" that characterizes a photograph; rather, they were aspiring to depict a different (and, to them, higher) sense of reality.

Apply this logic to the Renaissance. Just as the standards of the Renaissance cannot account for medieval art, so too modern standards cannot account for Renaissance worldviews. Whatever the Renaissance was, you can't portray it in a photograph. You must make a tapestry of it, or compose a sonnet, or write a romance, or dance a morris dance, or bait a bear. There is a reason why, as Proust says, the portraits of an era all look mysteriously alike. Every portrait incarnates that strange being known as the

Times. The only case in which we cannot perceive the thickness of the representational envelope is in the case of our own times.

Then, and only then, we think we are merely seeing things as they actually are, merely being realistic. What it means to us to be realistic seems, as though coincidentally, the same as to be photographic—as if the photographic medium were no medium at all, but a transparent window onto the way things simply are. We cannot see the look of the Times so long as we are in them. A man wearing yellow-tinted glasses ... &c.

•

Ships and Shipwrecks

Explorers traversing the wild sea, as depicted in André Thevet's 1575 *La Cosmographie Universelle*.

•

Images—a painting, a sculptural relief, a memory—may underlie the secret history of many books, but they play an especially important role in romance. For Aristotle, images are the raw material of thought: "The soul," he says, "never thinks without a mental image." Thought is the mind's dilated process of making sense of its images. They are the systolic contraction that pumps blood through the whole thinking apparatus. From an initial single image, thought fills out the implications, interprets, translates a tension into two or three or more characters, and then tells a story or makes an argument. Twentieth-century writers like Ernst Bloch, Siegfried Kracauer, and Adorno tried to theorize the generative power of what they called the *Denkbild*, or thought-image. Such an image, they said, expresses something for which there is no direct equivalent in words—and, perhaps because such an image won't be easily domesticated in the realm of words, creates friction and sets thought moving.

It may be that images are especially important to romance partly because this genre resists teleology—by which I mean only that romance wanders instead of, as epic does, building toward an end that is presented as fated and inevitable, like (presumably) the founding of Rome. Therefore, romance has to regenerate its momentum over and over. As one episodic adventure ends, romance has to find a way to begin again. One push will not get it from the first page to the last. Spenser uses images constantly in this way to restart his *Faerie Queene*. He is, according to Northrop Frye, "helpless without some kind of visualization to start him thinking." When he needs to begin again, he describes an emblematic figure of Patience or Jealousy, and then, to unfold the dilemmas that she embodies, he sets her going through an imaginary world, where she encounters other emblematic figures and interacts with them. Una, the personification of Unity, rides a white donkey and trails behind the brave knight; they enter the wandering wood, where he soon encounters and chops the head off Errour, a monster whose greedy spawn feeds from her bleeding wound . . .

Poetry thus becomes, as was said repeatedly in the Renaissance, a speaking picture.

•

Philip Sidney's younger sister, Mary, who helped revise the *Arcadia* after Philip died, was thirteen years old when she was sent to Elizabeth's court in 1575. Her sister Ambrosia, with whom she had often worn matching outfits, had recently died. In a consoling letter written to the girls' father, Queen Elizabeth herself invites Mary to court. At the head of the letter—as Margaret P. Hannay, her biographer, points out—the queen has crossed out the customary address of "Right trusty and wellbeloved" and added the more personal "Good Sidney." She reassures Sir Henry that he doesn't have to worry about Mary: "*We* [the royal plural] will have a special care of her."

It didn't take long before the thirteen-year-old witnessed truly lavish royal entertainment. That summer, in July, she accompanied Elizabeth to Kenilworth, a many-tiered limestone castle of a beguiling soft color that Hannay describes as a warm pinkish brown, and that reminds visitors of a sunset or—since limestone is, in fact, composed of ancient marine sediment like coral and mollusks—of a reef. Originally a Norman tower in the twelfth century, Kenilworth had been built and rebuilt by a succession of owners, so that it had grown over the centuries, and now housed the queen's favorite, Robert Dudley, Earl of Leicester, and his massive entourage. The queen stayed for nearly three weeks, the longest she would ever stay with a courtier, and the celebrations were elaborate. What characterizes this and many other Elizabethan festivities is the literary nature of the image-making and spectacle. In this case, the queen's visit included, as Hannay describes, "'accidental' encounters with allegorical personages on bridges or in holly bushes that made it seem as though the queen and her court were vacationing in Spenser's realm of Faerie." Hannay weaves into her prose a letter written by Robert Langham, who witnessed these events (she maintains the irregular spelling that is the norm for the period):

When Mary entered the park with the queen, she would have seen that "one of the ten Sibills . . . cumly clad in a pall of white

sylk, pronoounced a proper poezi in English ryme and meter."
The porter then came out, complaining of such noise and confusion as had never disturbed his courtyard—until he saw the
queen and made suitable reverence. Trumpeters, each with "hiz
sylvery Trumpet of a fyve foot long," sounded a welcome from
the wall of the gate. Elizabeth and her party crossed the tiltyard,
the Lady of the Lake floated near on her "moovabl Iland, bright
blazing with torches," welcoming the queen to her lake.

But Elizabeth was not one to be outdone—not even by a fictional
lady in the context of a tribute to herself—and took advantage of
the moment by reminding all onlookers of her own dominance:

> The queen thanked her [the Lady of the Lake], but added "we
> had thought indeed the Lake had been oours, and doo you call
> it yourz noow?"

•

Sidney provides a key for how to make aesthetic judgments
when you find yourself in a situation where someone has more
power than you do—that is, when you find yourself in this world.
In the *Arcadia*, he writes, "But she was a Queen, and therefore
beautiful."

•

It is recorded that, in the winter of 1581, Philip Sidney gave Queen Elizabeth a whip studded with diamonds as a New Year's gift. It is no coincidence that his first name is associated with the horse (ἵππος). Let there be no doubt who is the rider and who the ridden.

•

Here is an image that occurs early in Sidney's *Arcadia*:

> But a little way off they saw the mast, whose proud height now lay along, like a widow having lost her make [mate] of whom she held her honor; but upon the mast they saw a young man (at least if he were a man) bearing show of about eighteen years of age, who sat (as on horseback) having nothing upon him but his shirt, which being wrought with blue silk & gold, had a kind of resemblance to the sea, on which the sun (then near his Western home) did shoot some of his beams. His hair (which the young men of Greece used to wear very long) was stirred up & down with the wind, which seemed to have a sport to play with it, as the sea had to kiss his feet; himself full of admirable beauty,

set forth by the strangeness both of his seat & gesture: for, holding his head up full of unmoved majesty, he held a sword aloft with his fair arm, which often he waved about his crown as though he would threaten the world in that extremity.

This is a painting made out of words: a young man astride a mast wearing only a shirt of blue silk and gold. The phrase "at least if he were a man" suggests that, like Sidney himself, he's androgynous. (An early biographer, John Aubrey, describes Sidney's appearance: "He was not only of an excellent wit, but extremely beautiful; he much resembled his sister, but his hair was not red, but a little inclining, viz. a dark amber color. If I were to find a fault in it, methinks 'tis not masculine enough; yet he was a person of great courage.") Or perhaps he's not between a man and a woman, but between a man and a god. Or maybe, in his blue and golden shirt, he's the blue sea with the golden sun gleaming on it. Or maybe he's the wind (notice his long hair moving in the air). Or maybe he's a ship (like a billowing sail on a mast?). And, yet, like some kind of mirage over there in the distance, wavering in and out of being the whole world, merging with it, becoming one with it, he also asserts himself—waving his sword around his head "as though he would threaten the world in that extremity."

With all its parenthetical additions, this romance is a kind of magical box with many interior drawers. Amid all the mysterious images and events described throughout the *Arcadia*'s pages, the initial description of the young hero seems to be an object of wonder brought from a faraway land.

•

Ships were once controversial. Recall that they did not exist in the Golden Age, when, as Ovid puts it in Arthur Golding's sixteenth-century translation:

> The lofty pine-tree was not hewn from mountains, where it
> stood,
> In seeking strange and foreign lands to rove upon the flood;
> Men knew none other countries yet....

Early explorers must have experienced an internal sense of prohibition: when they blew through the Strait of Gibraltar, and entered into the vast chaotic swirl of the Atlantic, which swarmed at that time with monsters, they were traveling into unknown regions of the universe, maybe even into unknown regions of themselves. Dante consigns Odysseus to hell partly for

persuading his companions to sail with him beyond the Pillars of Hercules, beyond the natural limits of man. Montaigne didn't focus on ships, but also wanted people to stay put and plot their own gardens. Why won't human beings just be content with what they are, where they are, what they can know—rather than this constant fretting, roving, rifling, debating, justifying, quibbling, acquiring, tinkering, *sailing*?

—*Whatever*. My cat, rolling onto his back and stretching the length of his indolent body against the heat vent, concurs. Or at least, since he *truly* doesn't believe in the blah-blah of argument, has no objection. He still lives in that Golden Age, and for him there is no law, no labor, no strife or ambition, no winter, no money, no farming, no sailing. Gold-rimmed cans of Lap-of-Luxury simply appear in the sky. After making a little swish this way and that way (as is only natural, normal, and right), he watches as chunks of reconstituted meat product, the ground-up remains of horse noses and chicken toes, hover for a moment in glorious viscosity before sliding out of the Can and into the Bowl. Like snowflakes, no two chunks are exactly the same. Yes, my child, the world is bountiful and good.

•

Lamps at night are lighthouses of the imagination. Imagination goes and returns to them, gauges its distance on the sea of its own protean worlds by their peaceful and steady light. Or maybe, with their softly glowing golden shades, they are the planets of the domestic nighttime thought-world. Without needs of their own (not even the need to fall, as things on planets feel), they hover in space, quietly communicating to the mental seafarer their promise that something out there will remain unchanged—. They are the kindly gaze that searches your eyes for the pain it might take on itself—. The silence of the desk lamp is so profound that all sounds, except maybe the leaflike rustling of a turning page, or the animal scratching of the pen's nib, stay at a distance, hovering at the periphery of the luminous circle. A clink of a dish in the other room, a shuffle of a known pair of slippers, a faucet on, then off, a heating pipe—these sounds only increase the silence around the lamp. Around the lamp, the air becomes more still. Electrons settle down, and nuclei become like pillows. What is this mysterious harmony that a lamp has with a book? It is as if the lamp knew and shared in the silence that lies at the heart of the book, beneath all the eager little words.

> I slept before a wall of books and they
> calmed everything in the room, even
> their contents....
>
> —Saskia Hamilton, "*Zwijgen*"

Such lines are written in lamplight.

•

A new Sidney book (used) arrives in the mail. There are not many signs that the volume has been read, but on one page the previous owner has left two marks declaring her response:

How bold, how forthright a mind! What journeys occur in armchairs.

•

Suddenly putting his hand on his heart and bowing his head, the professor of another era said, "I am not embarrassed to say that at this point I feel a certain emotion—"

•

Worthy Gentlemen of the Academy, You have done me the honor of inviting me to present a report on my previous life as an ape.

Kafka's monkey is speaking to the academy, recalling that decisive moment of breakthrough when he first crossed the line that separates animal from human:

I called out "Halloo!", breaking into human sounds, and with this call made the leap into the human community. And its echo: "Listen, he's talking!" felt like a kiss over all my sweating body.

I repeat: there was no attraction for me in mimicking humans; I mimicked them because I was looking for a way out....

•

—But as I was saying:

—After much discussion and debate, Telemachos finally decides to set out in search of news about his father. It is as though his mind, having moved into itself, and further into itself, having shifted from indecision to decision, from decision to indecision, having wondered what was his problem that he would have to go back and forth like this, forth and back, over and over, having wept tears of frustration and shame before the elder men, having thrown the scepter onto the ground (*how like a child!*), having wandered from one internal mental chamber into another—until, suddenly, he makes his choice: he will search for news about his father. The goddess Athena urges him to follow this plan. In Telemachos's likeness, she then goes through the city, telling the men to assemble that evening by the ship, which she stocks with gear. Finally, she puts to sleep the suitors who might impede his voyage. All this happens so quickly that the goblets fall from the suitors' hands. Now all is ready. Only Telemachos's resolution is needed. Likening herself to Mentor, Athena goes to him and tells him that it is time, his companions are at the oars. She says, "So let us go, and not delay our voyaging longer." And so, just like that, he gets up and goes. Is it the "us" that has at last persuaded him? He follows the god, and the men follow him. And then, after all the indecision, it is happening: he is on the open sea with the bracing surf against his face—

> Telemachos . . . gave the sign and urged his companions
> to lay hold of the tackle, and they listened to his urging
> and, raising the mast pole made of fir, they set it upright
> in the hollow hole in the box, and made it fast with forestays,
> and with halyards strongly twisted of leather pulled up the
> white sails.

The wind blew into the middle of the sail, and at the
   cutwater
a blue wave rose and sang strongly as the ship went onward.
She ran swiftly, cutting across the swell her pathway.

The wind lifts, the waves surge, everything sings. Physical reality
rises to meet his will.

•

Even the best-documented Renaissance people appear only partly
in the historical record: whole decades of the lives of dukes and

 earls disappear into shadows.
For women, the record tends
to be even more fragmentary.
A letter or financial account
or wedding negotiation is the
single flash of lightning that
for an instant illuminates a
human being's whole world,
and then all is darkness again.
In the case of Philip Sidney's
grandmother on his mother's
side, Jane Guildford Dudley,

Duchess of Northumberland, lady-in-waiting of Anne Boleyn, intimate friend of Katherine Parr, one of the most complete statements we have from her is her final will, written shortly before her death in January 1555 at the age of forty-six. She had been educated by the great humanist Juan Luis Vives, and had deftly maneuvered to save her family after Mary Tudor swiftly executed her husband for his close connection with Mary's rival Lady Jane Grey (Lady Grey was married to the duke and duchess's son Guildford). Rising for a last moment from oblivion, what does Philip Sidney's grandmother say? She tells us who gets which gown. The one "with a high back of fair wrought Velvet" is for Philip's mother, Mary. Indeed, this gown may be the one that Mary Dudley is wearing in her Penshurst portrait. And then there's a clock to dispose of, a green velvet chair, a horse and saddle, a Turkish carpet. The Duchess of Alva gets the green parrot. Sidney's grandmother asks for mercy for her sons. And, whether from modesty or horror of violence, she expresses more than once her aversion to the dissection of her body after death: having "not loved to be very bold afore Women," she would be even more "loath to come into the hands of any living Man." Do not spend my money on my funeral, she asks; instead, consider my children and my servants; pay my debts. Wrap me up in a simple sheet. My body "is but meat for worms."

This is hardly the only case of a sixteenth-century woman

whose fullest surviving statement expresses the desire to efface her mortal being before God. Ironically, it is the expression of this desire to be nothing that momentarily conjures her worldly existence: her feelings about her body and her things. And so verbal are these people that, for just a moment, you can hear the very timbre of her voice—inflexible, suffering, and intelligent. And then that's all. The jaws of darkness close, and she's gone.

•

My other grandmother, my mother's mother, who was also from the Midwest, was intelligent and unusually articulate, with a quality of taut intention and humor, disrupted by some kind of inner turmoil that periodically broke forth. The terms of her struggle were almost entirely unknown to me, but her battles manifested sometimes in the fierce way that she performed simple gestures, like how she set a glass in front of a plate, abruptly slamming it down, exclaiming, "So! Shall we eat!" And nothing in the transcription of that statement can convey how harsh it sounded, almost like a curse. Occasionally, these inner battles manifested more extremely, bursting forth in sudden acts of semi-constrained violence, as when she slapped my mother across the face, hard—a blow so unexpected that none of us knew what was happening. It was as if lightning had struck a beloved tree.

Immediately afterward, my grandmother disappeared into her bedroom, where she stayed for the rest of the day, and the counterattacks of self-reproach and remorse that she suffered were evident in her puffy, weary face when she emerged the next morning. An inner life was for her a strictly private affair. Yet there was something painful in her heart that would build up and, against her will and understanding of her obligations, would periodically call out for release—and, to some extent, *find* release. While my grandfather's journals were logbooks that listed his expenditures, tallied the minutes he spent exercising, and tracked shifts of temperature and barometric pressure, my grandmother's journals recorded her thoughts—or so my mother's glimpses of a few pages had suggested. Once, during the night, when I was very young, I saw my grandmother on the way to the bathroom, with her hair partly down, and for just an instant, as in the sudden illumination from a flash of lightning (to return to that image), she looked completely different, wild, like John the Baptist emerging from the woods, but then almost immediately she was reaching back and pinning her hair up again and squinting her eyes at me in playful mock accusation. "Aha, it's the young criminal!" she exclaimed, and again she was the person I knew. Her favorite writer was Jane Austen, and after everyone had gone to bed, she would sit at the dining room table and reread late into the night *Persuasion* or *Sense and Sensibility*, propping open the book with a bowl of whipped cream. Into this bowl she would drop a single shelled pecan, which she would then, with a small spoon, scoop out—one pecan at a time. When I lay in bed at night in the guest room, I could sometimes hear the faint clink of her spoon against the side of the bowl.

•

My mother's parents disapproved of my father after he left us, but later, after my stepfather appeared, my father started to grow again in their esteem and seem, in retrospect, not so bad. At least he had a career. At least he had a job! My stepfather, meanwhile, was a borderland creature: unemployed, from Brooklyn, an artist (*sort of*), unassimilated, and he enjoyed his food a little too sincerely. It was polite to be appreciative of what was served, but he would lean over the plate of food and, wafting the steam up toward his face with one hand, would say, "Well, that smells just wonderful!"; then, eating, he would issue sounds: "Mmmmm-hmmmmm!" and "Ahhhhhhhhhh!" and "Deliccccciousssssss!" Perhaps these exclamations were rendered even more emphatic by his desire to be polite. My grandmother responded at first with a faint smile, but then, as this behavior continued, eventually just kept her eyes down and pretended not to notice. When we were done, my stepfather pushed back his chair and folded his hands across his midsection: "Now, *that*," he said, looking around at everyone at the table, "was a nice cut of meat!"

•

During her final years, which were very hard years, my maternal grandmother would sometimes seem to be writing with one finger in the air when she lay on her back in bed. Was she still writing her thoughts, I wonder, and still confiding them only to herself? It is said that all words are written, ultimately, in the sand, or, in this case, in the air—gone already like a breath. Borges tells a story about a man who is about to be executed. Facing the firing squad in the prison courtyard, he develops a full three-act play in the moment between when the commander orders that the executioners fire their rifles and when a bullet strikes his heart. In that instant, as the bullet should be flying toward him, time seems to stand still. Or perhaps the man's awareness of time has become so precise that the instant seems to last for a year. As he stands there, waiting for the bullet, he completes the entire play in hexameters, composing each line, one at a time, and bringing this piece of literature to the most exquisite completion. But this play can exist only for him alone, who, in the next instant, is gone.

•

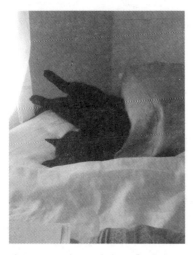

Two knights are dueling. Pretending to flee, Agricane leads Orlando into a lush glade by a fountain, where they continue to fight. The day drags on, the sun sinks down, but the knights are so well matched that neither can gain the upper hand. Soon the stars come out. Eventually, utterly exhausted, the knights can hardly lift their swords, and they find themselves lying in the verdant grass side by side, "like two men bound by ancient peace." Looking up at the stars overhead, Orlando begins to talk about God, but Agricane, who is Muslim, says that he does not want to argue over faith. He says that a nobleman shouldn't spend the whole day reading books, anyhow: "I did not want to learn when young." Learning is alright for priests and scribes, Agricane continues, but riding and hunting are right for him. Bleeding from his injuries through his shirt, Orlando agrees that "a man's first honors are in arms, but learning does not lessen men—it adds, like flowers in a field." Well, says Agricane, no matter. (This letters-versus-arms debate was all too well known in the Renaissance and was becoming tedious.) If Orlando wants to talk, Agricane says, they should talk about either (1) WAR or (2) LOVE. "Any knight who despises love lives heartless—he just looks alive," says Agricane, trying to get the conversation going again. And, more provokingly, isn't Orlando famous for being "*innamorato*"? (After all, that is the title of the poem in which they exist: Boiardo's romance *Orlando innamorato*.) Orlando explains that, yes, he's *innamorato* because he's in love with the beautiful Angelica. Agricane rages: With Angelica?! Burning with jealousy, he informs Orlando that he is the one truly in love with her. Soon, having caught their breath, the two knights resume their fighting in the pitch-black night.

•

Thus passes the glory of the world, sighs my mother, *sic transit gloria mundi*. She is sweeping up the shards of the old vase, the lovely one that she had bought in England with my father, shortly after their engagement. It had repeatedly fallen or maybe occasionally been thrown, and my stepfather had repaired it each time. For a long while, without handles, it had held the toothbrushes in the bathroom. *Oh!—damn*, my mother had said this final time, after accidentally knocking it off the sink. *You won't believe what I just did again!*

•

Opening the door to the reading room of an archive is maybe a kind of metaphor for opening the cover of a book, which is maybe a kind of a metaphor for entering one of the many chambers of the history of thought. For all its magnificence, the dark wood reading room of the Folger Shakespeare Library is no match for the wonder of what's housed here: thousands upon thousands of rare or unique documents from the Renaissance, patiently preserved, intelligently handled. Manuscripts, maps, early editions, ephemera. For me, long choosing and beginning late, entering the world of scholarship is like passing through a magic door.

•

If you work with archival manuscripts and old books, you learn almost immediately that not all the marks you find on the pages date from the time of publication. In regard to sixteenth-century texts, over four hundred years of readers have left their readerly graffiti. Readers have added manicules or written their thoughts in the margins; they have noted their expenditures and inscribed their names on the inside front cover; they have accidentally dripped candle wax on the pages, burned a corner. Collectors have rebound books, sometimes collating into one volume what was published at different times, even chopping the pages so that they fit the new binding; and some collectors have added their personal bookplates. Librarians of another era have glued typed tables of contents into the first or final pages. The pages also sometimes show damage from *before* publication. In the case of medieval manuscripts, for example, the vellum sometimes shows a wound to the animal whose skin has become the pages of the book: a tick bite in the calfskin can grow over time into a sizable hole in the text.

The room is cold, as probably were most rooms in the Renaissance. The dozen or so scholars working here today have piled knitted things around their necks, or pulled the strings of their hoodies tight. Seated in the privacy of their own pools of lamplight, these scholars work in a manner that appears attentive, sharp, and taut, sometimes almost athletic. Some of them stand, their faces hovering over their books. These scholars are talking with ghosts who are demanding interlocutors. A woman in a red turtleneck at a nearby table is examining a massive 1480s German Bible to find what words Luther may have changed when he made his 1522 translation. She has just discovered a single word that Luther appears to have altered. This observation, she thinks, will help retell the story of the Lutheran Bible, just ever so slightly. That will be her mark—tiny, precise, and, for her at least this afternoon, rich with implication. The smallest determination can, like a pair of longitude and latitude coordinates, indicate a new world. The observation is already rippling outward through the beautiful pools of knowledge in her mind. Among such scholars, it is impossible to separate selflessness from the self; her vast knowledge of Luther is, after all, the labor of her life's hours.

Today at the library, I am a hiker in a forest who, wandering, stumbles upon an arrangement of stones, or a bottle cap, or some other sign of another human having traveled this path. When I'm done, I close the Sidney manuscript, put it in its box, and return it to the archivist. She asks me whether I will need the text again tomorrow. "No, no, today is my last day," I tell her. "I'm going home tomorrow." She smiles in such a way as to communicate more than one gracious response at the same time: It was nice to have you here; I hope you will be returning again soon;

Did you find what you were looking for? I nod and try to recip-
rocate through the twitching of my eyebrows: Thank you so
much for your trouble; I found more than I was hoping to find,
more than I deserved to find; It's incredible what you do here;
I can't believe that somehow this wonderful place still exists; I am
not worthy; Have a good weekend.

Returning to my table to pack my things, I find, scattered on
the foam wedges, which are used as supports to avoid stressing
the bindings of frail books, these little bits of paper and thread:

These bits must have come off the Sidney manuscript during the
time I was examining it. This manuscript, even in its brief and
modest relationship with me, has broken down just a little further. Thus, says 1 John 2:17, "this world passeth away...."

•

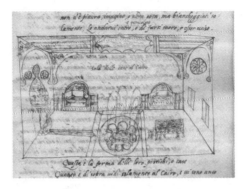

A girl was building a caravansary out of napkins and toothpicks. Lying on the rug, she worked with concentrated attention, arranging pennies to make a curving copper path to the water pit and then pushing the neck of the lamp lower to produce an effect of bright sun. Raising herself higher on her elbows to admire her work, she then chose a blue crayon, with which she carefully began to cover an entire sheet of paper. That was the sky. What's important to understand is that her backdrop did not *represent* the blue of the sky; rather, it *was* this blue. Although her blue was on a smaller scale, admittedly, it could nonetheless be considered in some ways superior to that of the sky because it did not recede as one approached it, but could be touched.

•

At the mention of ..., she smiled slightly, as though to herself, privately. At that moment, she was ... *tender*? *gentle*? *happy*? *thoughtful*? Yes, and as *remote* as a boat out on the sea.

•

"There is no hope which is not also in part a memory."

•

In the first book of the *Arcadia*, Pyrocles sees a picture of the beautiful Philoclea. He falls in love with her image and, as did so many young men in the Renaissance, soon slips into a pining *melancholia*. Just because it was a fashionable disease does not mean that it was not painful. Think of Romeo, whose very name sounds like a self-involved sigh, *oh me oh*; or recall Robert Burton's 1621 *Anatomy of Melancholy*, which attempts to delineate concisely the problem of melancholy in a thousand and some pages; or conjure before your mind's eye Albrecht Dürer's famous image *Melencolia I*. The most obvious symptom of this illness, writers agree, is the afflicted's desire to be alone. Burton's initial "Abstract of Melancholy" begins, "When I go musing all alone," and that is the very situation with Pyrocles: "Every morning early going abroad, either to the garden, or to some woods towards the desert, it seemed his only comfort was to be without a comforter." His bosom friend, his confidant, the brother of his heart, Musidorus (the one who, at the beginning of the book, spotted him riding the mast among the fragments of the shipwreck), finds him and tries to talk him out of this deplorable state with abundant, rhetorically elaborate, and unconvincing arguments against solitude (the enemy of virtuous action, &c.)—but to no avail. Finally, their host, the good Kalander, interrupts by inviting them on a hunt. ("*Nothing like good blood lust to cure depression*," interjects my mother when I read these pages to her on the telephone.)

As they head out into the woods, Kalander describes hunting trips he took when he was young. Back then, he says, even the moon could not "dissuade him from watching till midnight for the deer's feeding." (What is it about that image of waiting in the woods until midnight for the deer that already quickens the reader's fancy and pricks her ears?) "Oh," he continues, "you will never live to my age, without you keep yourselves in breath with exercise, and in heart with joyfulness: too much thinking doth consume the spirits: & oft it falls out, that while one thinks too much of his doing, he leaves to do the effect of his thinking." His message is clear enough: No more words. And as though to demonstrate the point, Kalander soon breaks off and unleashes the hounds. The hunt is on. Soon all is yelping, galloping, crashing, voices, and horns. When the stag is finally cornered, Kalander won't allow the young men to kill the deer with their swords. Rather, he "with a crossbow sent a death to the poor beast, who with tears showed the unkindness he took of man's cruelty." A hunt is, of course, all about a single-minded drive, a pursuit, a chase, and the hunt ends where it ends. After all, remarks the scholar Anne Lake Prescott, "deer are not wrong to tremble."

In blending sexual desire with hunting, this story follows a familiar pattern. In the anonymous medieval romance *Sir Gawain and the Green Knight*, to take another example, the lady of a castle tries to sexually seduce Gawain, the hero, while everyone else is away on a hunt. The scenes are intercut together: the lady's attempted seduction in Gawain's bedroom; the chase; Gawain's resistance to the lady in his bedroom; the kill. With the hooves pounding on the ground, and the heavy breath of the dogs, the hunt becomes what almost seems to have already happened—sex—but what in the end was resisted.

Prescott conjures the many examples needed to understand the literary history of eroticized deer hunts: Virgil (*Aeneid* 4.66–73), Horace (*Odes* 1.23), Petrarch (*Canzoniere* 190), Tasso ("Questa fera gentil"). Usually, the story is violent and ends with the deer's death—but not always. In the sixth lyric of Marguerite de Navarre's 1547 *Chansons spirituelles*, or here in Spenser's *Amoretti* 67, the deer allows herself to be captured:

Like as a huntsman after weary chase,
Seeing the game from him escaped away,
Sits down to rest him in some shady place,
With panting hounds beguiled of their prey:
So after long pursuit and vain assay,
When I all weary had the chase forsook,
The gentle deer returned the selfsame way,
Thinking to quench her thirst at the next brook.
There she beholding me with milder look,
Sought not to fly, but fearless still did bide,
Till I in hand her yet half trembling took,
And with her own good will her firmly tied.
Strange thing, me seemed, to see a beast so wild,
So goodly won, with her own will beguiled.

In this case, the deer submits—but does so by "her own good will," or at least by "her own will beguiled." She gives in, allows herself to be won, and takes upon herself, so Prescott says, a measure of suffering for the sake of a deeper fulfillment. The quest is erotic and (since the deer is also Christ) religious, both, inextricably.

Spenser's poem stages also a quest of literary interpretation—and such interpretation is after all not unerotic insofar as it deals with desire, with wish. Everyone who has ever really struggled for a long time to understand a text (her own or someone else's) knows this experience: After much strain and labor, and late nights, and early mornings, and foreign language classes, and discarded drafts, and frustration, and criticism, and embarrassment, and inability to explain the project to well-intentioned relatives, and huge tumbling piles of printouts, and self-doubt, and failure failure failure, you eventually give up the chase (but also don't give it up). You say, well, Fuck it.

...

...

...

And then suddenly, one afternoon, the text comes to you. Gently, on her little hooves, she picks her way to you through all the fallen leaves.

•

In his seventeenth-century *Brief Lives*, John Aubrey praises Philip Sidney for lifting poetry out of the darkness into which it had sunk. As an example of the bleak times before Sidney, Aubrey cites the anonymous *Pleasant Comoedie of Jacob and Esau*, which, he says, was performed before Henry VIII. Shaking his discerning head, our biographer recalls the profanity of this play by reciting this single line: "The pottage was so good, that God Almighty might have put his finger in't." This play, which has survived, has much discussion of pottage, but—it should be noted for the sake of scholarly accuracy—God considers putting his finger not in Abraham's pottage, but in his *broth*.

•

Flotsam and jetsam wash up on the shores of the mind. The same Aubrey recalls:

My great uncle, Mr. Thomas Browne, remembered him [Philip Sidney]; and said that he was often wont, as he was hunting on our pleasant plains, to take his table book out of his pocket, and write down his notions as they came into his head, when he was writing his *Arcadia* (which was never finished by him).

Montaigne also worked with the bits that floated his way: thoughts, scraps of reading, illnesses, journeys, falls off horses. And in our own era (more or less) Walter Benjamin, wandering among the ruins of modernity preserved in the Bibliothèque nationale de France, writes in his scholarly romance (of sorts), *The Arcades Project*, "What for  others are deviations are, for me, the data which determine my course." Or think of Virginia Woolf, who, on April 20, 1919, writes in her diary: "What sort of diary should I like mine to be? Something loose knit, & yet not slovenly, so elastic that it will embrace any thing, solemn, slight or beautiful that comes into my mind. I should like it to resemble some deep old desk, or capacious hold-all, in which one flings a mass of odds & ends without look-ing them through. I should like to come back, after a year or two, & find that the collection had sorted itself & refined itself & coalesced, as such deposits so mysteriously do, into a mould, trans-parent enough to reflect the light of our life, & yet steady, tranquil composed with the aloofness of a work of art." Thus, the bits of the

shipwreck of time, shimmering as they sink down to the ocean floor, eventually submit to the processes of nature and become part of its ecology. Algae covers the boot; crustaceans live inside it—the old dichotomy of nature and culture is, at last, overcome.

•

PRINCIPLES OF MENTAL ACCRETION

The picture below shows a page of Montaigne's own copy of

his *Essays*. He worked on his *Essays* for about twenty years, publishing several substantially different versions, most importantly in 1580 and in 1588. After he died in 1592, a copy of the 1588 version was found covered with his handwriting. The version of Montaigne that we read today is based on his copy of this 1588 version, with his many additions integrated into the text and sometimes marked with a little "c" above the new bits. What is curious about the difference between the various editions is how little Montaigne eliminated. When he worked on his *Essays*, he most often just added new material, inserting words, clauses, and paragraphs into the

essays that had already been published and also adding essays that were entirely new. He didn't renounce much; rather, he changed what he had already written by augmenting, qualifying, setting forth a contrary claim. This manner of working models one experience of our own growth and aging: when we feel an old grief, we find that—incredibly, after all these years—it is still there, but that this aspect of ourselves has become part of a shifting constellation, orbiting now on an outer ring of who we have become.

There are also other books that, like Montaigne's, have seemed capable of infinite expansion, books that seem to grow with the author and to end, to seem capable of ending, only when the author dies—in a sense, like a diary. Could Walter Benjamin's research on the *Arcades* ever have ended? No, the book could only have become more extensive; it could only have grown. At the heart of this infinitely expanding universe lies a resistance to intellectual hierarchy, by which we might centralize the country of our thoughts and appoint a higher-order thought as ruler. Romance's "and-then" structure is the literary manifestation of this resistance to subordinating one idea to a higher (and often more abstract) idea. Instead, in romance, one thought links with another thought, arm in arm, arm in arm, weaving through the field—and there is no king or teacher.

•

LAW OF GROWTH

The number of pages grows not in the manner of inorganic things like a tower, where one concrete unit is inevitably placed on top another, upward, but in the manner of something organic like a plant, where the new leaves emerge mysteriously from within what is already always there, unfurling from the very center of its own parts. Just as the leaf unfurls from the stem, so too do new words and ideas emerge from the words and paragraphs that are already there, any of which, seemingly, can grow and thereby become a new center.

LAW OF DECAY

H

Drd

p

J

O

Kl(

o

•

Speravi = (Latin) "I have hoped."

~~Speravi~~ = Philip Sidney's motto while he was reworking the *Arcadia*.

•

"The more superfluous physical labor is made by the development of technology, the more enthusiastically it is set up as a model for mental work, which must not be tempted . . . to draw any awkward conclusions." Rather, thinking should "'produce' something."

•

Here's an image of urban life: Walking through the dark hallways on our floor of the apartment building, I pass a kitchen door that's been propped open with the security chain looped at about eye level. Sounds of a family—rattling of dishes and talking—a TV on—and the smells of cooking. When I pass— which is just a brief second—no one's looking my way, but I have to be careful not to pause or to look too long. I try to keep the same pace as I pass, but for just a flash, as when illuminated train cars fly by at night, a whole world goes by. A teenage boy, standing with his back mostly toward me, holding a plate of food, pauses to look at the television as he lifts a fork to his mouth, and to one side there's a woman bending down to get something out of the refrigerator, turning her head slightly as she speaks to him—and then nothing.

•

Pisanello's *The Vision of Saint Eustace* is a fifteenth-century painting that is bejeweled with rich colors as in a Persian miniature. All the animals are doing animal things: a silver dog chases a hare;

a hound sniffs another dog's anus; this dog chastely lowers its tail and waits inquisitively; another hound sniffs the air; two little

brown dogs paw at the grass; a white bird flies through the air…
Onto this field, Saint Eustace has ridden, decked out in his blue-
and-gold gleaming finery because that is what a human animal
does if he can: adorn himself in splendor. And who can say
whether he does so because of nature or culture?

The momentum of the picture goes from left to right—and
this motion has, only now, been suspended. SEE: the lower right
hoof of Saint Eustace's horse pauses in the air. Against this
flow of creaturely life, the stag carrying the crucifix between his
horns confronts the future saint. The current of life, of innocent
or cruel creaturely embeddedness, has been INTERRUPTED.
The moment rises out of the flow of animal drive… Note that
the scroll at the bottom of the picture has been left blank. For
Augustine, the experience of understanding words in order
evokes the experience of human life stretched out, painfully, in
the sequence of time. We rush, he said, from birth to death pulled
by desire in an unrelenting chase. But then, occasionally, "in the
flash of a trembling glance," a different experience of time rup-
tures into the present, and we lift out of the flow of things to
glimpse—?

•

These lines are from a poem by Tu Fu (eighth century CE):

The brook flows in the darkness
Below the flower path. The thatched
Roof is crowned with constellations.
As we write the candles burn short.
Our wits grow sharp as swords while
The wine goes round. When the poem
Contest is ended, someone
Sings a song of the South. And
I think of my little boat,
And long to be on my way.

•

What would it mean to look at Pisanello's picture from the position of the present? To see overlaid onto this picture the eras that separate us, eras that settle not as dust does, obscuring the picture, but as glazes do, enriching the image as the light of thought refracts through multiple layers, making the image glow...

Here is one experience of refraction through layers. Think of the hour before the sun goes down and the light glows with unaccountable beauty, so golden and warm. Suddenly, everyone on the city street is for a moment transfigured, resurrected as an angel version of herself; even the indifferent office buildings appear as though newly arisen in the heavenly city, their mute concrete blocks suddenly rendered as soft and effulgent as the shingled feathers of Gabriel's wing, and every passerby with her shopping bags glows like Mary when, eyes cast down, she receives the news that God will condescend to an earthly form through her mortal body—all because the sun, as it slips down toward the horizon, is shining through the zillions and zillions of zooming atoms that constitute the layers of earthly atmosphere and pollution.

•

You have been living in the world of the *Arcadia* for a long time now (for about 850 pages if you have been reading one of the most readily available modern editions), and it is a peculiar sensation actually to finish this book—that is, if you ever *do* finish it . . .

Arguably, even the author himself never finished it.

Sidney wrote one version that has—as we would expect from a complete book—a beginning and an ending. But he then started to revise the story. This revised version is the one that, with some editorial adjustments, his friend Fulke Greville helped publish in 1590. The problem is that Sidney had revised only about half before dying of gangrene from a leg wound in 1586. This revision ends midsentence and thereby, like its dead author, is tragically *maimed*—or so suggested members of the Sidney circle, most notably Philip's sister, the Countess of Pembroke, who helped publish, in 1593, a mended version by stitching onto the revised first threeish books the nonrevised last twoish books. It is difficult to say, in hard scholarly fact, which of the now-three versions should be considered the most complete or most authoritative.

But the problems of making such determinations are even more complicated because the revised and unrevised versions don't quite match up, plotwise, so the Scottish poet William Alexander composed a narrative patch, which was published first separately as a "supplement" around 1617. This patch was then integrated into the 1621 edition of Sidney's *Arcadia*, which includes, at that crucial spot in the third book, Alexander's new twenty-page bit—in order, it seems, to spackle over that textual crack or to cobble over that hole or, to return to the image of the wounded body, to graft over that *scar* (which Alexander indeed calls that "unfortunate maim"). But this solution, too, proved awkward. Because the revised plot was (arguably) heading off in a somewhat different direction, Alexander had been forced to invent a rather clunky plot contraption to end a battle in which the characters are so well matched against each other that neither can best the other. The poet manages by imagining a sudden whirlwind that carries a character named Anaxius out of the battle. It is always somewhat awkward to draw on divine meteorological explanation—what the scholar Colleen Ruth Rosenfeld calls "the supernatural causality of a cloud."

Whatever the implausibility of that solution, without it, the revision ends midsentence—or more precisely, even worse, it ends at the close of a parenthetical explanation inserted into the middle of a sentence. In other words, the book doesn't end; rather, it seems to disappear into its own digressive tendencies. Anaxius (the redoubtable knight) has just leapt away from Zelmane (the Amazon who is actually the hero Pyrocles in disguise), when the reader encounters the following:

The last line of which, enlarged, looks like this:

Whereat aſhamed, (as hauiñg neuer done ſo much before in his life)

❉ ❉ ❉

…which, in modern spelling and orthography (where "u" becomes "v," and where what looks more or less like an "f" is an "s"), translates to this:

> Whereat ashamed, (as having never done so much before in his life)

And then that's it: no more words. Thus, oddly, the 1590 version sputters out.

The scholar Jenny C. Mann draws attention to those strange, final parentheses, which are so awkward that editors have removed them from almost all modern editions. However, parentheses are there and everywhere in Sidney's own *Arcadia*(s) because he is constantly inserting, digressing, wandering, qualifying, and in a thousand ways forestalling the end. His odd parentheses typify the meandering, deviating, corkscrew aspects of his style. Mann quotes the Victorian essayist Charles Lamb, who describes Sidney's prose in these terms: His prose "seems unwilling ever to leave off, weaving parenthesis within parenthesis." Indeed, the complaint of William Hazlitt and others was that, as Mann puts it, Sidney's prose "utterly refuses to come to the point."

The point is perhaps that Sidney's story refuses to come to the point, as Alexander seems to have understood. In a passage of Alexander's supplement to which Mann directs the reader's attention, the shepherd Philisides (who is commonly accepted as a stand-in for Philip Sidney himself, whose name his name resembles) puts the matter this way: "Death, the only period of all respects, doth dispense with a free speech." Death, in other words, is the final punctuation. Full stop.

I am reading Mann's account of Sidney's parenthetical style right now in the Rose Reading Room of the New York Public Library, where, tipping my head back, I stare for a moment at the Tiepolo-esque clouds painted on the ceiling (as you, reader, may do so, too, wherever you are reading, by turning back to look at the cover of this book that you are holding in your hands)

•

But eventually, whatever version of the *Arcadia* you are reading, and wherever you are reading it, the book does inevitably end—or at least you close its pages...

Perhaps, after you're done reading it, you keep the book near you for a while, on your bedside table or on the dining room table or on the pile of books near a favorite chair. You don't put the book away immediately, just as you might not put away immediately the bathing suit and shorts that, lounging as though poolside in the half-open suitcase, you took on a summer trip. The book becomes part of the flotsam and jetsam that float in and out with the tide of household clutter. You like to look at the book, catch glimpses of it, its worn pages curling a little upward at the corners, as new leaves unfurl toward the light.

Those books that live with us lead, in my experience, complex lives—continuing in their intimacy with us long after we have forgotten what they actually say. They become footrests, yoga blocks, paperweights, door props, drink holders. My copy of *The Tale of Genji* holds open the bedroom window in the summer. An exhibition catalogue of Cézanne's bathers leans against the living room window to keep it from rattling when the air conditioner is on. A diary with inspirational Tolstoy quotations has proven the perfect size to hold open the bathroom door that otherwise slowly rotates until it bangs, annoyingly, against the toilet (a not-unique problem of Manhattan apartments). A copy of Audre Lorde's *Zami* has ended up, I don't know why, among the cookbooks. My now-innumerable passwords—scrawled on scraps of paper—live in volume 1 of Julia Child's *Mastering the Art of French Cooking*, in a copy that was once owned by my maternal grandmother and that somehow, with its pattern of faded red-orange fleur-de-lis on the cover, looks to me *like her*, or like one of her sweaters; my paper scraps with garbled passwords now reside among brown splatters and burn marks that testify to her aspirations to make the Fowl in Lemon Jelly that will never be attempted again.

But none of this experience of household intimacy with books is new. In the fourteenth century, Petrarch wrote about his life with a handwritten book of Cicero's letters, which he had transcribed himself and which he kept leaning against a doorpost. One day, when he was passing the volume, the fringe of his gown caught on it, knocking it against his left leg just above the ankle. The next day, the same thing happened, and this scene repeated itself three or four times in subsequent days. The wound eventually became infected, and Petrarch was in ill health for a year. Reflecting on the experience in a 1360 letter to his friend Boccaccio, Petrarch joked: "You are right: those with whom we live on the most *intimate* terms are the ones who most often molest us." Deciding that Cicero resented being kept on the floor, Petrarch had by this time moved the book to a higher shelf.

Glancing at the faded green cover of my *Arcadia*, I find that my memory of the plot has already started to dim, to blur; the adventures are—even now—sliding into one another, and I can no longer keep track of the basics: Which hero disguised himself as the shepherd and which the Amazon? Wait, which one is in love with Pamela and which Philoclea? —*Shameful*. If I were teaching a class on this book, I would have already become my own worst student, complaining that I really did do the reading even if I can't say anything at all coherent about what happened. The text, it seems, has already started to float away from me, just as Woolf said it would, "into the thin air of limbo." It has become like a dream, or perhaps, as has been said of another pastoral (Shakespeare's *As You Like It*), like "a summer cloud which dissolves into the blue." My own notes, scrawled everywhere in the margins, already make little sense to me.

But even if I (or you?) can't remember the plot of this book, perhaps we will continue to feel something like its presence, as we might continue to feel the presence of a friend or girlfriend who has just left the room and even to hear the inflections of her voice. *See,* says the (living) poet Carl Phillips, "how the sky becomes the echo of what's flown through it."

•

Failed Arcadia 3

After a sufficient quantity of sugar, the circuits of my twelve-year-old brain begin to flash like the blinking lights of the video game screens. My jean pockets are full of hot quarters, and my best friend and I wander through the windowless passageways of the urban underworld called the Golden Dome. Sometimes I pause to watch the champions play. Their faces are turned away, so I watch what they watch, the screen, and I watch also their hands. One sweaty hand wipes itself on a pants leg before taking again the joystick and shaking it furiously, convulsively; the other hand rests on the button, and with one finger it fires fires fires at the enemy. Sometimes a small crowd assembles, children and adults mixed together, but usually the struggle is a private affair. Could there be a place established for children that more resembles a den of illicit sexuality than this underground world with its stained carpets? I can only imagine, if the high score preserved at the top of the screen were someday mine, the glory that would befall me. Such is our childhood pastoral, the Video Arcade, the distant descendant of Arcadia.

•

If a classroom discussion is going well, a student—let's say a shy one, who is leaning over her book and papers, with her elbows on the table—may start to feel a peculiar inner sensation, an

agitation, a kind of mental pressure. This pressure may become stronger as the class goes on, so strong that she may take the risk of trying to find an outlet for it in words. The agitation, once articulated, turns out to have been a thought—one which hovers for a moment before its existence is affirmed by nods and by the slight brightening in the eyes of those sitting nearby. Soon, others in the class are responding to her thought with words of their own. A conversation ensues that has turns and momentums that cannot be planned for. In such a conversation, everyone—why not express this observation as a law of human nature?—who listens carefully and expresses herself accurately is elevated. We seem to glimpse a new mode of being with other people; we feel our own innate capacities. Such experiences show us, in Proust's words, "what richness, what variety, is hidden unbeknownst to us within that great and unpenetrated and disheartening darkness of our soul which we take for emptiness and nothingness." Such experience, which can shape an art, can also be an element of what happens in a school. In her 1971 article "How Do You Describe a Sunset . . . ," Rebecca Ricc, who was an actor in an outreach theater troupe that taught in prisons and in nursing homes and in my first school, articulated the transformative potential of this kind of experience, which she believed should be available to everybody, as a "process of expansion" that occurs within a prison, a body, "a frame."

•

Clouds. The evidence suggests that there were clouds before the Renaissance, but they take on an entirely new character in this period. No longer are they carved out of stone, as they appear to be in medieval icons where Christ ascends into a jagged chiseled dome of the sky. Suddenly, in the Renaissance, clouds become impossibly soft, light, ephemeral.

A thing that is nothing.

A thing that is many things.

One side sharp, the other diffuse, a new kind of cloud suddenly appears in our sky. These clouds are always in the process of becoming something else; the light they hold verges toward change. For only this instant are they that particular luminous pink or gray or blue or gold. Clouds tell of the faraway and also— and this, too, feels like a new kind of breath and freedom and also new intimation of terror—the it-could-be-otherwise. Swirling in stop-action over the concrete world in which we live, clouds provide their silent commentary on those of us hurrying below in our cheap or expensive suits. Clouds stay still for us only as long as we look at them, but then, as soon as our mind wanders, they take on a new shape and become a different color.

The largely unknown American painter Jane Wilson, who grew up on a farm in Iowa and who lived most of her adult life in New York City, dying here at ninety in 2015, painted the sky from memory over and over, one massive skyscape after the next: clouds before a storm, clouds at midnight, clouds before dawn. "The idea of a world that is so stable that the light doesn't change is appalling to me," she said in an interview before she died.

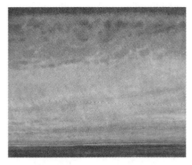

It has been said that if every thousand years there were only one sunrise (or was it sunset?) that is all anyone would talk about. Look at the shepherd in Poussin's painting on page 9. He leans on his staff and gazes while his goats continue to graze. Why do animals not look at clouds? Could this be a feature that characterizes the human—that we have a psychic need for clouds? At certain hours, even the people on the streets of New York look up.

Acknowledgments

To: Jeffrey Yang
Frances Mae White
Alaina Taylor
Timea Széll
Aoibheann Sweeney
Emily Sun
Sam Stoloff
Marty Sternin
Laura Slatkin
Joshua Scodel
Colleen R. Rosenfeld
Alice Quinn
Charles Perkins
Michael Murrin
Gael Mooney
Andrew Miller
Maureen McLane

ACKNOWLEDGMENTS

Hisham Matar
Diana Matar
Sara Kramer
Victoria Kahn
Heather James
Odile Hullot-Kentor
Saskia Hamilton
Achsah Guibbory
Amanda Gersten
Folger Institute
T. S. Eliot House
Betsy Eisendrath
Jeff Dolven
Julie Crawford
Valerie Cornell
Bradin Cormack
Christine Burgin
Linda Bell
Christopher Baswell
Barnard College (staff, faculty, & students)
Svetlana Alpers

Words adequate to you are lacking, but would have to be, as the painter demanded of his colors, "well arranged, resplendent."

Illustrations

Notes

5   *as Shakespeare's Adonis says*: *Venus and Adonis*, line 525, "Before I know myself seek not to know me," William Shakespeare, *Complete Sonnets and Poems*, ed. Colin Burrow (Oxford: Oxford University Press, 2002).

6   *"never lieth"*: Sir Philip Sidney, *An Apology for Poetry (or The Defence of Poesy)*, ed. Geoffrey Shepherd, revised R.W. Maslen (Manchester: Manchester University Press, 2002), 103.

7   *Shakespeare says in sonnet 104*: Shakespeare, *Complete Sonnets and Poems*, 104.2.

9   *C. S. Lewis said*: C. S. Lewis, *The Allegory of Love* (Cambridge: Cambridge University Press, 2013), 379.

10 *Jorge Luis Borges says*: Jorge Luis Borges, *This Craft of Verse*, ed. Călin-Andrei Mihăilescu (Cambridge, MA: Harvard University Press, 2000), 101–2.

10 *what Northrop Frye once called*: Northrop Frye, *The Myth of Deliverance*, reprinted in *Northrop Frye's Writings on Shakespeare and the Renaissance*, ed. Troni Y. Grande and Garry Sherbert (Toronto: University of Toronto Press, 2010), 362.

12   *"Virginia Woolf describes…"*: Virginia Woolf, "The Countess of Pembroke's Arcadia," in *The Second Common Reader*, ed. Andrew McNeillie (San Diego: Harcourt, 1986), 40.

14   *"For indeed, for severer eyes…"*: *The Prose Works of Sir Philip Sidney*, vol. 1, ed. Albert Feuillerat (Cambridge: Cambridge University Press, 1912), 3. All quotations of the *Arcadia* are from this edition. I have modernized the spelling and, occasionally, regularized the punctuation.

15   *we still have thirty-two engravings*: Alan Stewart, *Philip Sidney: A Double Life* (New York: St. Martin's Press, 2001), 1–8; John Aubrey, *Brief Lives*, vol. 2, ed. Andrew Clark (Oxford: Clarendon Press, 1898), 249–50. Spelling of Aubrey modernized.

15   *"I readily confess…"*: A. C. Hamilton, *Sir Philip Sidney: A Study of His Life and Works* (Cambridge: Cambridge University Press, 1977), 29; *The Correspondence of Sir Philip Sidney*, vol. 1, ed. Roger Kuin, (Oxford: Oxford University Press, 2012), 105–7.

19   *The intellectual historian Hans Blumenberg*: Hans Blumenberg, *Work on Myth*, trans. Robert M. Wallace (Cambridge, MA: MIT Press, 1985), 152.

19   *Johan Huizinga uncovered this dynamic*: Johan Huizinga, *The Autumn of the Middle Ages*, trans. Rodney J. Payton and Ulrich Mammitzsch (Chicago: University of Chicago Press, 1996), 1–2.

21   *"What is* pourquoi*?"*: William Shakespeare, *Twelfth Night*, ed. J. M. Lothian and T. W. Craik, Arden Shakespeare, 2nd series (London: Methuen, 1975), I.3.90.

21   *Theodor W. Adorno positions*: Theodor W. Adorno, *Aesthetic Theory*, ed. Gretel Adorno and Rolf Tiedemann, trans. Robert Hullot-Kentor (Minneapolis, MN: University of Minnesota Press, 1997), 119.

21 *"What are you for?"*: Shierry Weber Nicholsen, *Exact Imagination, Late Work: On Adorno's Aesthetics* (Cambridge, MA: MIT Press, 1997), 150.

22 *"be careful not to let..."*: *The Correspondence of Philip Sidney and Hubert Languet*, ed. William Aspenwall Bradley (Boston: Merrymount Press, 1912), 3–4.

22 *"You must consider..."*: Ibid., 28.

23 *"the very important matter..."*: Ibid., 22.

23 *"closest to the essentials of human nature"*: Cicero, *On Obligations*, trans. P. G. Walsh (Oxford: Oxford University Press, 2000), I.18.

23 *"devote too much energy..."*: Ibid., I.19.

23 *"turns in on itself"*: Ibid., I.156.

24 *"Oh," he wrote to Cicero*: Francesco Petrarch, *Letters on Familiar Matters (Rerum familiarum libri)*, vol. 3, trans. Aldo S. Bernardo (New York: Italica Press, 2005), XXIV.3.

25 *"acute frustration"*: F. J. Levy, "Philip Sidney Reconsidered," *English Literary Renaissance* 2.1 (Winter 1972): 12.

25 *"his end was not writing..."*: Greville quoted in ibid., 6. Spelling and punctuation modernized.

25 *"I have not as yet..."*: *The Correspondence of Philip Sidney and Hubert Languet*, ed. Bradley, 160.

26 *"Let us see..."*: Ibid.

26 *"Do you not see..."*: Ibid.

29 *This little hand-drawn picture*: William H. Sherman, *Used Books: Marking Readers in Renaissance England* (Philadelphia, PA: University of Pennsylvania Press, 2008), 37.

29 *"cull some flowers"*: *The Correspondence of Sir Philip Sidney*, vol. I, ed. Kuin, 34.

29 *a compendium of rhetorical examples*: See, for example, Abraham Fraunce's *The Arcadian Rhetorike* (London: Thomas Orwin, 1588).

30 *"We often find..."*: Desiderius Erasmus, "The Treatise *De Ratione Studii*, that is, *Upon the Right Method of Instruction*," in William Harrison Woodward, *Desiderius Erasmus: Concerning the Aim and Method of Education* (Cambridge: Cambridge University Press, 1904), 162.

31 *"the* thing's *the thing"*: Jonathan Gil Harris, introduction to Thomas Dekker, *The Shoemaker's Holiday* (London: Bloomsbury, 2008), xiii.

31 *"Words in themselves delight him..."*: Woolf, *The Second Common Reader*, 43.

31 *"We have come to long..."*: Ibid., 48–49.

33 *"breath of garlic-eaters"*: William Shakespeare, *Coriolanus*, ed. Peter Holland, Arden Shakespeare, 3rd series (London: Bloomsbury, 2013), IV.6.97. Menenius is describing ancient Roman plebeians, but Shakespeare, in creating this character, is drawing on attitudes of his own day.

33 *"apron-men"*: Ibid., IV.6.99.

34 *"It implies a protest..."*: Theodor W. Adorno, "On Lyric Poetry and Society," in *Notes to Literature*, vol. 1, ed. Rolf Tiedemann, trans. Shierry Weber Nicholsen (New York: Columbia University Press, 1991), 39–40.

34 *"This was the Golden Age..."*: Ovid, *Metamorphoses*, trans. Anthony S. Kline (Ann Arbor, MI: Borders Classics, 2004), 5.

35 *"This is a nation..."*: Michel de Montaigne, "Of Cannibals," in *The Complete Works: Essays, Travel Journal, Letters*, trans. Donald M. Frame (New York: Knopf, 2003), 186. All citations of Montaigne from this edition.

35 *Winsor McCay had based*: John Canemaker, *Winsor McCay: His Life and Art* (Boca Raton, FL: CRC Press, 2018), 108.

37 *"Paris is in the hands…"*: *The Diary of Virginia Woolf*, vol. 5 (1936–1941), ed. Anne Olivier Bell (San Diego: Harcourt Brace Jovanovich, 1984), 296–97.

39 *"There was something historically absurd…"*: Leonard Woolf, *The Journey Not the Arrival Matters: An Autobiography of the Years 1939 to 1969* (New York: Harcourt, Brace & World, 1969), 57–58. Quoted in Natania Rosenfeld, *Outsiders Together: Virginia and Leonard Woolf* (Princeton, NJ: Princeton University Press, 2000), 14.

41 *The term, which a painter taught me*: The painter is Graham Nickson, the dean of the New York Studio School.

42 *"tragedy, comedy, history…"*: From the 1623 Folio edition cited in *Hamlet*, ed. Ann Thompson and Neil Taylor, Arden Shakespeare, 3rd series (London: Thomson, 2006), II.2.334–35.

42 *"trumpery"*: William Shakespeare, *The Winter's Tale*, ed. John Pitcher, Arden Shakespeare, 3rd series (London: Bloomsbury, 2010), IV.4.602.

43 *"But gentlemen, these cony-catchers…"*: Robert Greene, *The Second and Last Part of Cony-Catching*, 1592. Renascence Editions, available at www.luminarium.org/renascence-editions/greene4.html. Spelling and punctuation modernized.

44 *"Is it true, think you?"*: Shakespeare, *The Winter's Tale*, IV.4.266–67.

44 *"Pray now, buy some…"*: Ibid., IV.4.260–61. Italics mine.

45 *"It was in the time…"*: *The Prose Works of Sir Philip Sidney*, 5.

45 *"Though he were naked…"*: Ibid., 8.

46 Elaborate *is a late sixteenth-century word*: *Oxford English Dictionary*, "elaborate," adj., II.2.

46 *"They are the lords and owners..."*: Shakespeare, *Complete Sonnets and Poems*, 94.7.

46 *Montaigne describes the visit*: Montaigne, "Of Cannibals," in *The Complete Works*, 193.

48 *When he and his men got off the boat*: For an account of this voyage and for a transcription and translation of this letter, see Lawrence C. Wroth, *The Voyages of Giovanni da Verrazzano, 1524–1528* (New Haven, CT: Yale University Press, 1970).

49 *The name* Arcadia: *Oxford English Dictionary*, *Acadian*, n. and adj., etymology.

49 *"There is nothing so insipid..."*: Montaigne, "Of Experience," in *The Complete Works*, 1043.

50 *"Yea, I am a very babe..."*: Katherine Parr, *Complete Works and Correspondence*, ed. Janel Mueller (Chicago: University of Chicago Press, 2011), 282.

51 *He focuses, for example, on Rabelais's neologisms*: Leo Spitzer, *Linguistics and Literary History: Essays in Stylistics* (Princeton, NJ: Princeton University Press, 1948), 15–17.

51 *"creates word-families..."*: Ibid., 17.

52 *Ben Jonson typifies this development*: Jonas A. Barish, *Ben Jonson and the Language of Prose Comedy* (Cambridge, MA: Harvard University Press, 1960).

52 *"soft and precise enunciation..."*: Thomas H. English, "Biographical Note" in Morris W. Croll, *Style, Rhetoric, and Rhythm*, ed. J. Max Patrick and Robert O. Evans (Princeton, NJ: Princeton University Press, 1966), ix.

53 *"similarities or repetitions of sound..."*: Croll, *Style, Rhetoric, and Rhythm*, 54.

53 *"the sensuous character of its appeal…"*: Ibid., 56.

55 *"Each member is as short…"*: Ibid., 212.

56 *"But the sense is much altered…"*: George Puttenham, *The Art of English Poesy: A Critical Edition*, ed. Frank Whigham and Wayne A. Rebhorn (Ithaca, NY: Cornell University Press, 2007), 267.

60 *Torquato Tasso shows his hero Rinaldo*: Torquato Tasso, *Jerusalem Delivered (Gerusalemme liberata)*, ed. and trans. Anthony M. Esolen (Baltimore, MD: Johns Hopkins University Press, 2000), xvi.

61 *"But all those pleasant bowers…"*: Edmund Spenser, *The Faerie Queene*, ed. A. C. Hamilton, Hiroshi Yamashita, Toshiyuki Suzuki, and Shohachi Fukuda (Harlow, UK: Longman, Pearson Education, 2007), II.xii.83. I have modernized Spenser's spelling.

61 *readers have long noticed the quality of self-repression*: See Stephen Greenblatt, *Renaissance Self-Fashioning: From More to Shakespeare* (Chicago: University of Chicago Press, 1980), 172–75.

61 *Adorno and Horkheimer would consider this*: Max Horkheimer and Theodor W. Adorno, *Dialectic of Enlightenment: Philosophical Fragments*, ed. Gunzelin Schmid Noerr, trans. Edmund Jephcott (Stanford, CA: Stanford University Press, 2002).

62 *Vivian Gordon Harsh*: Donald Franklin Joyce, "Vivian G. Harsh Collection of Afro-American History and Literature, Chicago Public Library," *The Library Quarterly: Information, Community, Policy* 58.1 (January 1988): 67–74; and www.blackpast.org/african-american-history/harsh-vivian-gordon-1890-1960/. Thanks to Laura Helton and Beth Loch.

63 *"He ran toward the group…"*: Steven Yaccino and Catrin Einhorn, "Chicago Girl's Shooting Death Jolts City and Touches Capital," *The New York Times*, January 31, 2013, A13.

63 *After her death, her Latin teacher wrote*: Mark Datema Lipscomb, "Teaching Latin and the Second Amendment," *The Progressive Populist* (March 15, 2013), www.populist.com/16.05.lipscomb.html.

67 *"all agree that it began…"*: Pliny, *Natural History*, vol. 9, books 33–35, trans. H. Rackham (Cambridge, MA: Loeb Classical Library, 1952), XXXV.5.

69 *"The literal is barbaric"*: Adorno, *Aesthetic Theory*, 61.

69 *He points out that the chambers of memory*: Augustine, *Confessions*, trans. Henry Chadwick (Oxford: Oxford University Press, 1991), X.15.

70 *Borges says that…*: Borges, *This Craft of Verse*, 10.

70 *There was once a monk*: John Cassian's story of Sarapion and its context from Mary Carruthers, *The Craft of Thought: Meditation, Rhetoric, and the Making of Images, 400–1200* (Cambridge: Cambridge University Press, 1998), 70–72.

70 *"apprehended by the eye or seized by the mind"*: John Cassian, *The Conferences*, trans. Boniface Ramsey, O.P. (New York: Newman Press, 1997), 372.

71 *"And then amid these prayers…"*: Cassian quoted in Carruthers, *The Craft of Thought*, 71.

76 *"like a boy of 18"*: Thomas Mann, *Pro and Contra Wagner*, trans. Allan Blunden (Chicago: University of Chicago Press, 1985), 211.

77 *the story that Herodotus tells*: Herodotus, *Histories*, I.8–13.

78 *"to see the issue"*: Shakespeare, *The Winter's Tale*, V.3.128.

78 *"I am for you again"*: Ibid., II.1.22.

79 *"No other Odysseus than I…"*: Homer, *The Odyssey*, trans. Richmond Lattimore (New York: Harper, 1975), XVI.204.

79   *Plotinus praised the Egyptians*: Plotinus, *The Enneads*, trans. Stephen MacKenna (London: Penguin, 1991), V.8.6.

80   *"with one glance of its mind"*: Boethius, *The Consolation of Philosophy*, trans. H. F. Stewart (Cambridge, MA: Loeb Classical Library, 1973), V.6.83–84.

80   *the front and two sides*: Erle Loran, *Cézanne's Compositions: Analysis of His Form with Diagrams and Photographs of His Motifs* (Berkeley, CA: University of California Press, 1943).

80   *as Proust says, the portraits of an era*: Marcel Proust, *Swann's Way*, trans. Lydia Davis (New York: Penguin Books, 2003), 20. Thanks to Elisabeth Ladenson.

83   *"The soul," he says, "never thinks..."*: Aristotle, *On the Soul; Parva Naturalia; On Breath*, trans. W. S. Hett (Cambridge, MA: Loeb Classical Library, 1957), 431a17.

83   *Twentieth-century writers like*: Gerhard Richter, *Thought-Images: Frankfurt School Writers' Reflections from Damaged Life* (Stanford, CA: Stanford University Press, 2007), especially 12–13.

83   *"helpless without some kind of visualization..."*: Northrop Frye, "The Structure of Imagery in *The Faerie Queene*," reprinted in *Northrop Frye's Writings on Shakespeare and the Renaissance*, 56.

84   *Her sister Ambrosia*: For discussion of Ambrosia's death and for quotations from Queen Elizabeth's letter inviting Mary to her court, see Margaret P. Hannay, *Philip's Phoenix: Mary Sidney, Countess of Pembroke* (Oxford: Oxford University Press, 1990), 31. Spelling modernized.

85   *she accompanied Elizabeth to Kenilworth*: Ibid., 33.

85   *"'accidental' encounters with allegorical personages..."*: Ibid., 34.

85   *"When Mary entered the park..."*: Ibid.

86   *"The queen thanked her…"*: Ibid.

86   *"But she was a Queen…"*: *The Prose Works of Sir Philip Sidney*, 103.

87   *"But a little way off…"*: Ibid., 10.

88   *"He was not only…"*: Aubrey, *Brief Lives*, 247.

89   *"The lofty pine-tree…"*: Ovid, *Ovid's Metamorphoses*, trans. Arthur Golding, ed. Madeleine Forey (Baltimore, MD: Johns Hopkins University Press, 2002), I.109–11.

89   *Dante consigns Odysseus to hell*: Dante, *Inferno*, XXVI.103ff.

92   *"I slept before a wall of books…"*: Saskia Hamilton, "*Zwijgen*," in *Corridor* (Minneapolis, MN: Graywolf Press, 2014), 46.

93   *"I am not embarrassed to say…"*: Theodor W. Adorno, *Lectures on Negative Dialectics*, ed. Rolf Tiedemann, trans. Rodney Livingstone (Malden, MA: Polity Press, 2008), 38.

94   "Worthy Gentlemen of the Academy…": Franz Kafka, "A Report to an Academy," in *A Hunger Artist and Other Stories*, trans. Joyce Crick (Oxford: Oxford University Press, 2012), 37.

94   *"I called out…"*: Ibid., 44.

95   *"So let us go…"*: Homer, *The Odyssey*, II.404.

95   *"Telemachos…gave the sign"*: Ibid., II.422–29.

97   *Rising for a last moment from oblivion*: On Jane Dudley's will, see Hannay, *Philip's Phoenix*, 8–9; also, Simon Adams, *Leicester and the Court: Essays on Elizabethan Politics* (Manchester: Manchester University Press, 2002), 134.

101 *Borges tells a story*: Jorge Luis Borges, "The Secret Miracle," in *Collected Fictions*, trans. Andrew Hurley (New York: Penguin, 1998), 157–62.

102 *Two knights are dueling*: Matteo Maria Boiardo, *Orlando Innamorato (Orlando in Love)*, trans. Charles Stanley Ross (West Lafayette, IN: Parlor Press, 2004), I.18.39–55.

105 *In the case of medieval manuscripts*: Thanks to Christopher Baswell.

109 *"There is no hope…"*: Simon Jarvis, *Adorno: A Critical Introduction* (New York: Routledge, 1998), 231.

109 *"When I go musing all alone"*: Robert Burton, *The Anatomy of Melancholy*, ed. Holbrook Jackson (New York: New York Review Books, 2001), 11.

109 *"Every morning early going…"*: *The Prose Works of Sir Philip Sidney*, 54.

110 *"dissuade him from watching…"*: Ibid., 59–60.

111 *"with a crossbow sent a death…"*: Ibid., 61.

111 *"deer are not wrong to tremble"*: Anne Lake Prescott, "The Thirsty Deer and the Lord of Life: Some Contexts for *Amoretti* 67–70," *Spenser Studies* 6 (1986): 33–76.

112 *"Like as a huntsman…"*: *The Yale Edition of the Shorter Poems of Edmund Spenser*, ed. William A. Oram et al. (New Haven, CT: Yale University Press, 1989), 640–41. Spelling modernized.

114 *"The pottage was so good…"*: Aubrey, *Brief Lives*, 248.

115 *"My great uncle, Mr. Thomas Browne…"*: Ibid.

115 *"What for others are deviations…"*: Walter Benjamin, *The Arcades Project*, ed. Rolf Tiedemann, trans. Howard Eiland and Kevin McLaughlin (Cambridge, MA: Belknap Press of Harvard University Press, 1999), 456.

115 *"What sort of diary…"*: *The Diary of Virginia Woolf*, vol. 1 (1915–1919), ed. Anne Olivier Bell (New York: Harcourt Brace Jovanovich, 1977), 266.

119 *Just as the leaf unfurls*: See Johann Wolfgang von Goethe, *The Metamorphosis of Plants* (Kimberton, PA: Bio-Dynamic Farming and Gardening Association, Inc., 1993).

120 *Speravi*: Sidney bore a shield with this device during a court tournament in 1581. For the device's possible reference to his dashed hopes for inheritance, as well as other disappointments, see Hamilton, *Sir Philip Sidney*, 3; also, Joan Rees, *Sir Philip Sidney and* Arcadia (Rutherford, NJ: Fairleigh Dickinson University Press, 1991), 14.

120 *"The more superfluous…"*: Horkheimer and Adorno, *Dialectic of Enlightenment*, 167.

122 *"in the flash of a trembling glance"*: Augustine, *Confessions*, VII.17.

123 *"The brook flows in the darkness…"*: Tu Fu, "Banquet at the Tso Family Manor," in *One Hundred Poems from the Chinese*, trans. Kenneth Rexroth (New York: New Directions, 1971), 3.

125 *Scottish poet William Alexander*: Gavin Alexander, *Writing After Sidney: The Literary Response to Sir Philip Sidney 1586–1640* (Oxford: Oxford University Press, 2006), 273.

125 *"unfortunate maim"*: Colleen Ruth Rosenfeld, *Indecorous Thinking: Figures of Speech in Early Modern Poetics* (New York: Fordham University Press, 2018), 122.

125 *"the supernatural causality of a cloud"*: Ibid.

127 *"seems unwilling ever to leave off…"*: Jenny C. Mann, *Outlaw Rhetoric: Figuring Vernacular Eloquence in Shakespeare's England* (Ithaca, NY: Cornell University Press, 2012), 101.

127 *"utterly refuses to come to the point"*: Ibid., 103.

128 *"Death, the only period…"*: Ibid.., 113.

130 *"You are right…"*: Petrarch's 1360 letter to Boccaccio is quoted in Leo Spitzer, "The Problem of Latin Renaissance Poetry," *Studies in the Renaissance* 2 (1955): 124. Italics mine. For this story of the Cicero volume that wounded Petrarch, see also Petrarch, *Letters on Familiar Matters*, XXI.10.

131 *"a summer cloud which dissolves…"*: Walter Benjamin, *Gesammelte Schriften*, vol. 2, ed. Rolf Tiedemann and Hermann Schweppenhäuser (Frankfurt am Main: Suhrkamp, 1972), 611, quoted in Julia Reinhard Lupton, "Shakespeare's *Sturm*, Caliban's *Drang*: Walter Benjamin and *The Tempest*," in *Political Aesthetics in the Era of Shakespeare*, ed. Christopher Pye (Evanston, IL: Northwestern University Press, 2020), 267.

131 *"how the sky becomes the echo…"*: Carl Phillips, "Brace of Antlers," *Silverchest* (New York: Farrar, Straus and Giroux, 2013), 48.

133 *"what richness, what variety…"*: Proust, *Swann's Way*, trans. Lydia Davis, 363.

133 *"process of expansion"*: Becky [Rebecca] Rice, "How Do You Describe a Sunset…To Someone Who's Never Seen One," *Off Our Backs* 1.23 (June 1971): 9.

134 *"The idea of a world…"*: Elizabeth Barlow Rogers, "In the Studio with Jane," DC Moore Gallery catalogue for Jane Wilson show, January 5–February 10, 2007, 7.

138 *"well arranged, resplendent"*: Vincent van Gogh, letter to his sister Wilhelmina J. van Gogh, September 1888, *The Complete Letters of Vincent van Gogh*, vol. 3 (Greenwich, CT: New York Graphic Society, 1959), 444.

RACHEL EISENDRATH is a critic and scholar who specializes in English Renaissance poetry. The author of *Poetry in a World of Things* (winner of the 2019 Elizabeth Dietz Award), she is the Tow Associate Professor of English and director of the Medieval and Renaissance Studies Program at Barnard College in New York City.